Tales of a Bear Hunter

Tales of a Bear Hunter

by

Dalton Carr

SAFARI PRESS INC.

The trademark Safari Press ® is registered with the U.S. Patent and Trademark Office and in other countries.

Carr, Dalton

Safari Press Inc.

2001, Long Beach, California

ISBN 1-57157-171-X

Library of Congress Catalog Card Number: 99-066844

10 9 8 7 6 5 4 3 2

Printed in the U.S.A.

Readers wishing to receive the Safari Press catalog, featuring many fine books on big-game hunting, wingshooting, and sporting firearms, should write to Safari Press Inc., P.O. Box 3095, Long Beach, CA 90803, USA. Tel: (714) 894-9080 or visit our Web site at www.safaripress.com.

Dedication

This book is dedicated to three people.

First, my loving wife, Anne, who never complained about my countless hunting trips. To my long-suffering wife I wish to say, "I love you."

Second, C. E. Barnett, to whom I credit most of my education concerning bears. He was the greatest bear hunter I have ever known.

Third, Lloyd Carr, my father, who taught me many things about hunting bear. Moreover, he taught me how to be a man and the relationship of bear to man, which only an experienced woodsman can know. He is the only man I have ever feared and the man I loved the most.

Acknowledgments

I want to thank my wife, Anne. Because I have Parkinson's disease, I had to dictate the entire manuscript to her. Anne also helped me when I 'hit a brick wall' during my dictation. She is a real godsend. Without her efforts this book probably would never have seen print.

Sonja Laab labored day and night to complete the first typewritten manuscript, and I thank her so much for her efforts. Larry Kaniut, author of *Alaska Bear Tales* I and II and *Some Bears Kill,* edited my first copy and suggested additional changes that proved invaluable. Ikey Starks at Sports West in Denver, Colorado, helped me put together the chapter on rifles and cartridges. An expert gunsmith, Ikey has a great deal of insight into the problems that arise with certain rifle actions. Jane Hume was kind enough to provide illustrations for the book. Thank you, Jane.

There are others who have contributed in the preparation of the manuscript, such as Eddie Gunyon, Dick Sanders, "Bear" Turner, Chuck Taylor, Robert Aaberg, Bill Moon, Jim Hasler, Jan Roth, Lynn Bellville, and Kevin and Wanda Brown. They are all bear hunters and they are all my friends. Thanks for the memories. I'll never forget any of you.

Table of Contents

Foreword

I first met Dalton Carr in 1993. He told me then that he was writing a book about his 41 years as a bear hunter, and he wondered if I would read the manuscript when it was completed. I agreed. Over the years he kept me informed of his progress, which was hampered by Dalton's having Parkinson's disease. Last week he telephoned to say that he would be mailing me the completed manuscript.

Even though I've researched three books about bears, interviewing hundreds of bear-attack victims as well as many rescuers and bear experts, Dalton's book provided me with a lot of new information. But that is not all. Dalton's love of nature and respect for bears are reflected in the book's wonderful stories, particularly those in the chapters "The Bear with Personality" and "Spirit Bear." In the chapter "Huckleberry Bear," Dalton reminds us that a great hunt does not necessarily end in a kill. He also writes about fatherhood, describing in the chapter titled "Keith and the Three Bears" the special moments he and his son, Keith, shared during the boy's first encounters with bears.

Dalton's law enforcement background and his many years of big-game hunting have sharpened his observation skills, which is why this book is packed with astute details about wildlife. His knowledge of bear behavior is helpful to anyone venturing into bruin country, and the hunter will also benefit from Dalton's knowledge of bear anatomy and his discussion of the best cartridges and calibers for bear hunting.

Entertaining and informative, *Tales of a Bear Hunter* reveals not only Dalton's bear knowledge, but also his love for one of the most dangerous animals on earth. Enjoy the book. It's a dandy.

Larry Kaniut
Anchorage, Alaska
April 1999

Preface

Dalton Carr has been one of my best friends for fifteen years, but even before our friendship began I had heard of his prowess as a bear hunter. Indeed, perhaps I should call him *Mr.* Carr, the formal way Dalton often addressed his friend C. E. Barnett, who in Dalton's estimation was the greatest of all bear hunters.

What makes this book unique is that its author enjoyed a special affinity with bears. After all, who else but Dalton could share a fish and a campfire with a bear, or end his hunting career (as predicted by an old shaman) in pursuit of the wiliest of bruins. Since I joined Dalton on a few of the hunts for that wily "Spirit Bear," the chapter that recounts those hunts has for me a special poignancy.

When bear hunting, Dalton never used dogs or traps, always showing the greatest respect for his furry antagonist. He has also not related all of his most dramatic bear encounters in the book. Indeed, *Tales of a Bear Hunter* could be a lot longer, but since the volume is difficult to put down, who would get any sleep?

Dalton Carr is a natural storyteller with a phenomenal memory for detail. Live long and prosper, Mr. Carr. The world is waiting for more.

Jan Roth, Ph.D.
Craig, Colorado
April 1999

The First Bear

I can't rightly remember when I first felt the symptoms. They came upon me subtly, without my being aware. I also must have been quite young, for they have been with me for as long as I can remember. I have a name for the symptoms—bear fever!

When I was a boy, my dad, uncles, and their hunting buddies told bear tales around campfires. But the tales didn't remain only by the fire—they resurfaced in conversations at home during supper and while relaxing in the living room on long winter evenings.

Hearing bear tales told and retold throughout my boyhood years, I gradually learned quite a bit about bears—much that was fact and, yes, much that I discovered later to be fiction. Nevertheless, hardly a day went by that I didn't pretend I was Daniel Boone, Davy Crockett, or Hugh Glass tracking some mysterious and mighty bruin. Truth be known, there was more than one scrawny tomcat or black woolly puppy stung on its backside by a well-aimed BB of mine while I was in pursuit of a silvertip in the great Rocky Mountains.

As I grew older my enthusiasm remained, though I was surprised to discover that bear hunting was considerably more expensive and far more difficult than I had thought.

Furthermore, bear hunting is dangerous, which brings me to the story of my first bear hunt.

Dad and I were camping with three friends—Archie McCoy, Paul Culp, and Ted Hinton—on Alder Creek near the head of Poncha Pass, which is about twenty miles northwest of Salida, Colorado. Alder Creek meanders toward Baldy Mountain, which is a short distance from the old ghost town called Bonanza. All of us had tags for hunting deer, elk, and bear.

Until then I had seen six or seven bear, but only while involved in other pursuits such as fishing, berry picking, or the time-honored pastime of mountain loafing. I dreamed of hunting bear but still did not have a bear license.

Finally, I received the precious license and began to hunt the critter, armed with a hunting knife, a Winchester .30-30, and a Colt .45 Single Action. Experienced bear hunters may laugh at my .30-30, calling it an inadequate bear rifle. They would be surprised to learn that I have killed four bear, seven elk, and seventeen deer with that rifle—all before discovering that it was supposedly inadequate.

On the opening day of bear season, my hunting companions and I arose before sunup. I remember having a delicious breakfast, which is how breakfast usually tastes when you're eighteen years old and going hunting in the mountains. There was excitement at the breakfast table, too: Paul threatened to shoot Archie for cutting open cans of Vienna sausage with his razor-sharp hunting knife!

After breakfast, Paul and Archie (both of whom had made up by now) and Ted left camp and traveled up Alder Creek, while Dad and I worked our way up to the second ridge and then up an incline to Baldy Mountain. Sunlight broke over the ridge, beginning the process of melting the October night's heavy frost. For a mile Dad and I traveled a ridge line that headed almost due north. On the southwest side of the ridge there was a meadow with glorious patches of multicolored aspens sprinkled with occasional spruce. The northeast side of the ridge was almost covered with spruce. We planned to hunt for elk along the meadow at timber's edge until 10 A.M. and then hunt in the heavy evergreen forests until midday.

At 8 A.M. we heard a shot far down in the canyon. It sounded as if it were almost a mile away. The report had the sharp crack of a small caliber, not the *boom* of a larger high-powered rifle. Dad commented that it sounded like a .25-20 or .32-20, both of which are barely adequate for deer and illegal to hunt bear with.

The next two hours were fairly uneventful, except for our seeing numerous doe and a few cow elk lingering at the edge of the meadow. We also saw several two-point bucks, one of which was still sporting horns in half-velvet. None of these creatures, however, were really worth shooting for pot or trophy.

We approached a saddle approximately sixty yards long, with aspen timber covering the left side and spruce covering the right, forming something of a dividing line through the saddle's center. I was in the lead, about ten yards ahead of my dad. We frequently hunted this way, with the man in the rear watching the back-trail for any sneaky buck that might circle in behind. The aspen timber was dense with golden leaves; very little light penetrated its canopy.

I was surprised when I heard myself say, "There's a bear!"

"So I see," whispered Dad.

We had always said that in the event we encountered a bear—a large bear—Dad would shoot first with his .30-40 Krag and its heavier 220-grain bullet. I was debating whether to shoot when I saw the bear lower its head, extend its lips, and roll its ears back so tightly to its head that they seemed to disappear. These are indications that the bear is preparing to charge. It was then that I decided to shoot. I was applying pressure to the rifle's trigger when I heard the report of my father's Krag.

Spinning wildly away from the hit, the bear roared in pain and its jaws snapped frantically at its wound. Because of its whirling motion, Dad and I found it impossible to deliver the killing shot. The bear continued to snap at the wound, hooking right and left, its paws breaking four-inch-thick aspens as if they were toothpicks. Its wild gyrations took it down the hill about seven yards, and then it disappeared into a depression where the hillside turned to slough. I started advancing toward the depression with one eye looking down the rifle sights. Dad was behind me, saying firmly but calmly, "Careful, careful, careful." I looked into the depression and saw the bear directly below me. It was trying to raise itself up on its hind legs, its right foreleg hanging limply at its side. A bloody froth ran from the bear's mouth and onto its chest and belly fur. With the rifle muzzle a scant five feet from the bear's head, I touched the trigger and sent a 170-grain bullet straight into its brain. It sank slowly to the forest floor.

I couldn't believe my eyes! The great bear lying at my feet was awesome and, at the same time, sad to behold. Dad joined me on the edge of the slough, and both of us stood there a moment admiring the giant beast. Dad put his arm around my shoulder and said softly, "That's the biggest black bear I've ever seen, and he's your first. What a dandy."

I noticed that Dad's legs were trembling slightly. I then became aware that my own legs were trembling so badly that my knees were actually bumping together. Dad and I were experiencing what is called an adrenaline rush.

I was also aware of tears streaming down my cheeks—not from fear but from joy. Until a hunter experiences the rush that accompanies an encounter with a great omnivore, he will never know the elation of which I speak.

It was the greatest thrill and the greatest moment of many great moments I experienced while hunting with my father. I remember it as if it were yesterday: the envy on our friends' faces when they saw the great bear, and the pride my dad and I felt after killing such a ferocious animal.

Oh, yes! The bear! How could I forget! Field dressed, it weighed 460 pounds, a truly enormous creature. But why was it so cranky? We found the answer when we skinned it. Two hunters, both of whom were about my age, had seen the bear that day and one of them had taken a shot, which was what we had heard in the canyon. The shot penetrated about four inches into the bear's fat, settling in a muscle. Its meager penetration is something I will never forget. Naturally, having a bullet buried inside it didn't help the bear's disposition, causing it to prepare for a charge when it saw my father and me.

Even though it's 179 bears later, I still remember my first bear kill as the greatest thrill I've had in 41 years of bear hunting. But I cannot take all the credit; my bullet merely finished the inevitable. The success of my first hunt was largely due to my dad.

Grizzly for Breakfast

A lot of people think they are experts on what bears will or won't do. A while back, I read in a book the following statistics: 1 in 15 grizzlies, 1 in 20 Alaska brown bears, and 1 in 30 black bears will attack. (Yeah, I know, grizzlies and browns are supposed to be the same bear—more on that later.) I personally don't think anyone really knows when a bear will or won't attack.

I believe strongly that bear charges never occur without provocation. But the problem is that what constitutes provocation to a bear may not be recognized as provocation by a human being. I have experienced eleven charges by blacks and four by grizzlies. Without exception, all were provoked—some intentionally and some inadvertently. When meeting a bear at close quarters, the only prediction one can make with certainty is that the bear may or may not charge. The one in the following story did, and it was provoked considerably.

The elk camp between Jackson and Dubois, Wyoming, is usually easy to travel to a few days before opening day in mid-October. But on the previous night an early blizzard hit the Rockies. Snow fell for three days and nights, and winds blew up to forty miles per hour. Though skies cleared on the morning of the fourth day, the temperature at camp dropped to a bone-chilling minus 35 degrees.

Dad and I were hunting guides for six elk hunters from Davenport, Iowa. We lodged at a cozy cabin that had a fireplace at each end and walls doubly thick. Though we had remained snug throughout the blizzard, we were anxious to start the storm-delayed hunt.

The morning routine at the elk camp began with Dad starting the fire and putting on the coffee. I was usually the second one up, and that morning was no exception. After I said something about how cold the floor felt, Dad said, "Well, put your boots on and hustle in some of that kindling stacked on the porch."

Mumbling to myself, I pulled up my Levi's, slipped my suspenders over my shoulders, and slipped on my boots. Bracing myself for the cold, I opened the cabin door and stepped out onto the porch to be greeted by a beautifully clear, piercingly cold mountain morning.

To tell what happened next requires me to first explain the layout of the cabin's front porch and also a cold-weather custom of high-country people. The porch was about thirty-five feet long and nine feet wide. The eaves of the roof extended over the porch rail about four feet, protecting the porch from snowdrifts, and the porch rail was usually lined with saddles. When it is extremely cold, it is the custom to leave one's rifle in the scabbard rather than carry it into a warm house. Guns, when brought indoors after being subjected to subzero temperatures, immediately develop condensation on their metal parts, which can cause the parts to rust. This bit of mountain trivia explains why my rifle was still in the scabbard when the incident occurred.

The temperature at the time was about minus 20 degrees. After taking in the beautiful panorama created by the newly fallen snow, I started splitting wood for ten or twelve minutes. Now and then I looked up but saw nothing out of the ordinary. Dad started yelling from inside the cabin, "Wood's getting low. Hurry up." I split a few more chunks and had four armfuls to take inside when I heard several ponies inside the barn neigh and snort almost in unison. When I looked toward the barn, about fifty yards away, I was startled to see a sizable grizzly trying to climb the front gate of the rail fence about thirty-five yards from the front of the house. My mouth hung wide open. Though we had had grizzlies in camp before, this was the first time I had seen one this late in fall. Since the weather had been relatively warm before the blizzard, I gathered that this bear had been caught unprepared for hibernation.

What occurred next is etched in my memory in slow motion, like a scene from a Sam Peckinpah movie. The grizzly lost its footing twice on the snow-covered rail, then humorously jammed its nose and head about a foot and a half in the snow. It let out a *woof*, shook itself, and slapped the offending rail as if to say, "There, take that!"

While observing this, I began to notice that the grizzly was wearing a mighty fine fur coat that would sure look good on the living room wall! By the way, grizzly shooting was legal in Wyoming at the time and I had a license.

While the bear was trying to climb over the fence, I stepped to the porch rail, pulled the cover off my saddle scabbard, and hauled out my .30-30. As you will remember from the previous chapter, I thought pretty highly of that little rifle, so with no further thought I aimed at the silvertip bruin. My sights lined up perfectly on Old Griz's forehead. I smoothly squeezed the trigger.

BOOM! The bullet smacked the bear right where I'd aimed, knocking it backward off the fence. It lay there just long enough for me to start patting myself on the back. Then, with explosive quickness that cannot be adequately described, the bear was on its feet and climbing the fence with unbelievable alacrity. I could see a bloody slash extending from between the bear's eyes to the top of its skull, and I realized the bullet had hit its skull at an oblique angle, causing the bullet to glance off.

Needless to say, the bear was no longer in a good mood. Its wails, woofs, and the snapping of its jaws filled the crystal clear mountain air. Blood from its scalp wound and saliva from its jaws flew in every direction. The bear, its head swinging from side to side, made straight for the porch. I think something like "Oh, heck!" (but probably something stronger) flashed through my mind about that time. I knew that my little rifle had failed me and that I was in very deep trouble. I had only three steps to the door, but it seemed to take forever to get there.

Once inside the cabin, I threw down my .30-30 and peeked through the door at the mad bear. I knew my dad's Model 86 Winchester in .45-90 would be the first rifle in the rack by the cabin door. I snatched it, and while standing in the doorway, I cocked the hammer and squeezed the trigger just as the bear reached the top step.

What is strange is that I clearly remember hearing the brass hit the floor a split second after the shot fired. In that moment of no return, my senses were fully aware.

The grizzly's head slammed to the porch with such force that blood from the prior scalp wound shot forward with such momentum that it sprayed me from head to toe. I backed into the cabin working the lever. The bear was spread out on the steps exactly like a rug, its eyes still open and a small curl of steam drifting upward from the purplish bullet hole that was a little left of and above its right eye. I relaxed. I knew it was over. The bear was dead.

Suddenly the adrenaline hit and the shakes began. Dad was standing by the stove, unable to see out the door, but he must have known what had happened. With his usual cool he asked, "Was it a big one?"

"Big enough, I guess!" I replied.

Dad handed me a cup of coffee and said, "Sit down before you fall down."

I sat down, shaking so badly I could hardly get the cup to my mouth. One of the clients edged up to the cabin door but was afraid to look outside. "Nha, wha, wha, what's happening, Carr?" he stammered.

Dad, still nonplussed, said, "Grizzly, unless I miss my guess."

With grim determination, the client finally managed to look around the doorframe. He stood for almost a minute, mouth agape and eyes bulging. He then asked the sixty-four-thousand-dollar question: "What would have happened if that grizzly had gotten inside the cabin?"

Dad walked over to him, handed him a cup of hot coffee, looked him squarely in the eye, and replied: "Well, I guess Old Griz would have had us for breakfast."

The end of the story is rather anticlimactic, but I will tell it anyway because some lessons may be learned.

First, don't shoot grizzly bears with an inadequate rifle! If the bullet from the .30-30 had hit the bear straight-on, it would have entered the creature's brain and done the job, but that also means the shot would have had to be perfect. The .45-90 loaded with 350-grainers had far more power than the .30-30 with its 170-grain loading. This enabled the rifle shot not only to penetrate the frontal plate of the bear's skull, but also to penetrate through its head, neck, and chest, exiting just below the rib cage.

Second, don't wound a grizzly without expecting instant retaliation if it believes you are the source of its pain. This was the first time I had observed the incredible speed with which a grizzly can travel from point A to point B. I would estimate that from when the first bullet hit to the moment the mortal shot was fired, the elapsed time couldn't have been more than six to eight seconds. In that time, the bear covered a good twenty-five yards! It is probably better not to broach what might have occurred had the bear made it into the cabin. With its wound and its body pumped full of adrenaline, God only knows the damage that would have been inflicted in a small room with eight people! To say the result would have been terrible would be an understatement.

By the way, our clients, the elk hunters, were afraid to leave the cabin without being accompanied. We couldn't convince them that this was not an everyday happening. We tried to explain that we usually saw only one or two grizzlies during the entire season and none had ever created serious problems before. In their defense, however, I know how I would've felt if I had been in their shoes. The elk hunters left camp with the mayhem of one bad bear seared in their memory.

Finally, some words about the bear. It was an eleven-year-old female in prime condition. It had no suckling cubs and was not pregnant. The only reason it climbed the fence was to find something to eat. Because of the stillness of the air, my scent had not reached it. If it had, the creature probably would have headed for the tall timber. I've noticed on several other occasions that the sound of chopping wood does not necessarily deter a bear from coming close, but human scent will deter it almost every time. We certainly can't blame the bear for the attack. A bullet to the head from a .30-30 would make anybody angry.

Huckleberry Bear

Hunting bears is exciting, challenging, and sometimes just plain fun. Most bear hunts, including those for predatory bear, do not end in a kill. The hunter spends many, many hours glassing hillsides and forests and in blinds without ever getting a shot at a bear. Indeed, after reading the first two chapters you might think bruins lurk behind every bush. This is simply not the case. Bear hunting without dogs and traps is the most demanding type of hunting. The expert deer or elk hunter will seldom bag one of the "wise old men" of the woods. Being a successful deer or elk hunter does not automatically make one a successful hunter of bears.

To be successful, you must have intimate knowledge of the bear's behavior, habits, and diet. You will have to know what the bear is feeding on at specific times of the year and at specific times of the day, and you must also know its sleeping and foraging habits. In short, you have to know more about the bear than it knows about you, and this level of intimacy requires many hours of observing and studying the bruin.

An old Indian saying goes something like this: If you put a man and a bear in four acres of heavy woods for a month, the man may see the bear one time, and if he is a good hunter, he may see the bear four or five times. But you can rest assured the bear will see the man every day. This is completely true; however, there are times when the hunter may simply get lucky, everything going his way. The following story is an example.

I once worked as predator control hunter at the Yakima Indian Reservation, located in the Cascade Mountains in Washington State, with C. E. Barnett, a great bear hunter and a trapper with the American Fish and Wildlife Service. Since the areas we worked overlapped, we often worked together to control predatory bears picking off sheep that grazed the reservation's meadows.

C. E. and I had to travel to Adams Lake, where several Basque sheepherders, living near the lake, had lost sheep to predatory bears. As we flew into the Adams Lake area, I noticed its breathtaking beauty, which is difficult to describe. The lake is nestled in a relatively wide valley that gradually becomes narrower at its northwest end, as though the valley were being pinched around the lake. On the east side of the lake there is a high rocky ridge covered with broken talus, sheer walls, and gigantic fallen rocks. On the west side the valley slopes toward the timber on Mount Adams.

The morning was cool, clear, and very still. There was a touch of frost on the meadow grass, and as the sun topped the skyline, its rays—shimmering on the frosted grass—gave the area a fairy-tale appearance. C. E. said, "I'll take the left side of the lake and you take the right side. Don't forget, the two bears are both black. One is about two hundred eighty-five pounds and has a club foot on the left front leg. The other is almost three hundred fifty pounds and has a white patch on its chest. Don't shoot any other bears unless you spot a trophy you can't resist."

C. E. made that last remark because there were about thirty bears living around the lake. The two bears we were after had killed thirty-six sheep from the first of June to the end of August, making them the two most wanted bears in the valley. Once our plane landed, C. E. and I parted company and the hunt was on!

On both sides of Adams Lake, huckleberry bushes were everywhere that day. Lightly nipped by an early September frost, the huckleberries were ripening nicely, making a tasty treat for bear and hunter. Every year I made a solemn oath not to overindulge on this delicious feast, but whenever at Adams Lake during summer I would weaken at the sight of all those berries. Like my New Year's resolutions, the oath didn't last long and I was soon stuffing my mouth with them.

I knew that the best vantage point would be high on the rocky wall overlooking the valley. Munching berries, I proceeded to the base of the wall. I started the treacherous climb at about 10 A.M. and then traveled along a narrow trail, where one false step could mean a two-hundred-foot fall to the rocks below.

At 11:30, I saw a jutting piece of talus the size of the top of a grand piano. It lay flat on the edge of an overhang overlooking the huckleberry patches below. I set up my spotting scope and started glassing for the two predators. By two in the afternoon I'd glassed over eleven bears in the valley, all of which were gobbling down huge quantities of huckleberries. I still hadn't been able to locate "Club Foot" or "Patch" and was beginning to suffer from eyestrain.

Then, immediately above me, a rock about the size of a bushel basket bounced down the hillside, followed by several smaller stones. Since there was no danger of their hitting me, and slides are not uncommon on ridges covered with talus, I was not unduly alarmed. I was, however, curious enough to look up to investigate why the first rock had dislodged.

About two hundred fifty yards up the 35-degree slope, I saw, much to my surprise, a bear looking down at me. I picked up my rifle, a brand new Mark-V in .300 Weatherby, and took a look through the 2X10 Imperial scope. As I slipped off the safety, I saw the bear clearly, for a split second, as it turned back into the rocks. The left front paw of the creature turned in awkwardly. It was Club Foot.

I repositioned myself on my small perch to get a shot at this black magician who had just pulled an admirable disappearing act. I realized it was hopeless trying to get above the bear, for I knew my scent would drift up the rocky face to tell it my every move. I decided to leave off hunting Club Foot for now and returned to glassing the valley. There was no use filling the air with invectives; Old Club Foot had outsmarted me and that was that.

By 3 P.M. the sun was beginning to go down behind the mountain skyline. I knew I had at least four and a half hours of light left, though now the valley would be in shadow, making spotting far more difficult. I then saw about seven hundred yards away a very large bear that I estimated weighed very nearly five hundred pounds. It outsized every other bear I'd seen in that area by better than a hundred pounds!

I thought of C. E.'s admonition about not killing any other bear unless I saw one I really wanted. This particular bruin was the largest I'd seen since arriving in Washington State two and a half years ago. I decided I just had to have it, so I started a long careful stalk to about two hundred and fifty yards. I knew if I got close enough I could place a shot that would kill the bear instantly. I had my work cut out for me, though, because the distance I had to cover was open ground almost all the way to where I intended to take my shot. For the next three hours, I crawled on hands and knees and sometimes flat on my belly, trying to close the gap on that berry-munchin' bear.

Every fifty yards I'd take a squint through the rifle's scope. I was now within three hundred yards and, much to my surprise, began to develop a fondness for the critter. It was certainly enjoying itself. It was so stuffed with berries that when it finished one bush it would roll to the next one. The bear could hardly wiggle!

At a hundred yards I was close enough to see its sleepy eyes, its berry-stained tongue, and what seemed to be a smile. I slipped off the safety and waited for the right opportunity. The bear rolled onto its back, pulling a berry branch to its chest with one paw and, with incredible finesse, nibbled the big black berries one at a time. Its other paw lay across its big round tummy. I settled the cross hairs just under its chin and started the pressure on the pound-and-a-half trigger pull that would send a 180-grain Nosler at 3200 feet per second into its spine near the skull.

The bear looked in my direction, though I knew it couldn't see me, and it looked so content and happy with the world. My last iota of resolve disappeared. I took my finger off of the trigger, slipped the safety back on, and smiled.

Now, if you think the hunt was over, you are wrong. The breeze was still blowing in my face, so I decided to see how close I could get to the happy diner. I spent the next thirty minutes crawling inch by inch to within fifteen yards. Then a really dastardly plan came to mind. I figured if the bear could make me crawl six hundred yards on hand, knee, and belly, the least I could do was have the last laugh. I was pretty well shielded from it by berry bushes and the breeze was still in my favor, so I felt safe in raising my camo-clad head to take a peek. The bear was still gobbling berries. I sat for probably three or four minutes, enjoying the view of the bear enjoying the berries. Then in a low voice I said, "Hey."

The bear, lying on its back, was a most comical sight—with front paws across its tummy, a surprised look on its face, its ears pricked forward, and its soft black nose rotating gently like a radar screen, trying to pick up a scent. The creature still wasn't sure if it had heard a human voice and it sat there ever so still. "Hey!" I said again. "Whatcha doin', big boy?"

With amusing swiftness, the bear leaped to its feet, let out a *woof,* and took off on a dead run, leaving a stream of huckleberry leavings behind it. Being such a big bear, it's a good thing its dead run wasn't in my direction!

The bear ran flat out over the horizon, and that was the last I saw of it. On the flight home, C. E. had me repeat the story several times, and each time we laughed harder and harder. C. E. kept saying, "I would give anything to have seen the look on that bear's face!"

The bear's priceless expression is forever imprinted in my memory, and I've had so much fun telling the story at hunting camps to fellow hunters. It seems that some of the best hunts, requiring the most skill and perseverance, don't always result in a kill. The memory wouldn't be nearly as good—or entertaining—if I had pulled the trigger.

Who's Afraid of the Dark?

I was in my early teens when I first read *Man-eaters of Kumaon*, Colonel Jim Corbett's great book on predatory tigers and leopards. Over the years I haven't lost my enthusiasm for Corbett's tales. Whenever I read of how he sat in a tree stand all night while a leopard tried to push past the blackthorn stave barricade, I feel goose bumps and the hairs standing up on the back of my neck. Hunting is then reduced to its most elemental form. If the hunter makes a mistake or fires a bad shot, he can die for his error. Rightly speaking, it is not so much being afraid of the dark as being afraid of what is in the darkness.

One of the best methods for killing a predator is by setting up a blind near a recently killed carcass, for a predator will likely return to finish its meal. This type of hunting would be relatively easy if the predator would return during daylight hours; most of the time, it returns under the cover of darkness. Consequently, the hunter spends many boring hours in the dark, sometimes capped off by the moment of terror when the killer returns. As one becomes more experienced in this type of hunting, the terror becomes mixed with nerve-tingling excitement.

Bait hunting requires a great deal of patience, and being a little crazy doesn't hurt either. Lying in the dark twenty-five yards from a bear's food supply, knowing that when it returns you might be its dessert, is not for everybody. But as far as I'm concerned, no other hunting method is quite as exciting, so let's examine this method closely.

An animal killed by bear may be left exactly where the attack took place or it may be dragged for some distance. If a bear intends to return to its prey, it will cover its kill with sticks and debris. The bear will then climb onto the pile and urinate, making claim to the carcass underneath. Rarely will any animal, other than a wolverine or tiny weasel, dare to invade the bear's larder. If the bear intends to soon return to the carcass, it may, rather than bury it, lie close by, guarding its prize. It behooves the hunter to take great care when approaching the general area of the kill.

A sheepherder or cattleman will often know the location of the last depredation, but that doesn't mean the carcass will be there. (My assumption that a bear's kill would still be in the same place very nearly cost me my life, but that story must wait till chapter 6.) The bear may drag the animal's body into deep cover, or it may leave it in the open. All this has to be ascertained and taken into consideration. It is wise not to move a carcass or disturb the area around it. It is also wise to know how air currents are flowing during the time you intend to sit near the bait. Pick a spot neither above nor below the air stream; make sure it's directly against the airflow and not more than thirty-five yards distant. Give yourself clear visibility without disturbing too much vegetation.

I usually bring a sheet or tarp, and with the aid of branches taken from the area, I make a lean-to that is seven-by-seven feet with a fourteen-inch slit in the wall facing the target. Made properly, the lean-to becomes a thoroughly camouflaged blind.

I understand that in Africa, lions will still come to bait sites where men have left a great deal of their scent. This is not true with bears. If possible, do not handle the bait at all, and leave as little scent in the area as possible. I have tried deer scent, pine scent, and virtually every other kind of scent known to man—all with questionable results. I've also tried mountain lion scent, thinking a bear wouldn't intentionally stalk a mountain lion. I was right. The scent didn't attract bears. It did, however, attract a male lion with amorous intent. I had one heck of a time getting myself out of that situation!

When I tried using bear scent, it either frightened the returning bear away or made it highly aggressive toward a would-be intruder. I finally decided on the most lowly of all scents— skunk! No animal is afraid of the skunk, but none wants to be sprayed by it either. Wearing skunk takes some time to get used to, but it really works. You should avoid wearing scented deodorant, aftershave lotion, or other cosmetic products into the blind. You should also wear clean clothes that, I hope, will still be odor-free when you come out.

I recommend entering the blind at least an hour before dark. You should have already strung a clear monofilament fish line from the bait to your position under the tarp. Other items you will need are a good five-cell flashlight loaded with fresh batteries, a rifle of adequate caliber, a customized bracket that attaches the flashlight to the rifle, and clothes heavy enough to ward off the early morning chill. Pick a comfortable position, tie the monofilament line to your left wrist, and wait. Avoid urinating or defecating within a hundred yards of the blind. If you have to eat during the vigil, eat a dry cereal. Do not eat pastries, cheese, or meat products, or you might end up with a very hungry bear for a dinner partner.

I mentioned that you need an adequate rifle. Remember, in all likelihood you are going to have only one shot at very close range and with minimal artificial lighting on the target. It is mandatory that your rifle be powerful enough to kill the bear with one shot.

A good bear rifle should be at least .333 bore and should be shooting something like a 225-grain bullet weight at a velocity of 2400 feet per second. The little .358 Winchester is a marvelous killer of bear that weigh up to three hundred pounds, but falls a little shy of optimum performance for anything larger. The best rifles for shooting bear over bait are the .338-06 and .338 Winchester Magnum, .340 Weatherby, .35 Whelen, .350 Remington Magnum, .358 Norma Magnum, and the great .375 H&H. I personally don't care for the .378 Weatherby Magnum unless it is loaded down somewhat in velocity, for it tends to have excessive expansion (which disintegrates the bullet, meaning the bullet can't penetrate sufficiently) at close range. I think the .416 in any of its many cartridge designations and the .458 Winchester would be ideal for hunting Alaska brownies, but since I've never heard of using them to shoot brown bear over night baits, the question is rather a moot one.

The two rifles I used extensively over night baits were the .338 and the .375, both with 20-inch barrels and aperture sights. The .338 is on an FN Mauser action, while the .375 is a Pre-'64 Winchester Model 70. Both rifles are super. I have used one or the other in 46 of my kills—and all were one-shot stoppers. You can't ask for more than that!

Low-power telescope sights may help, but I personally don't like to use any type of magnification when I am that close to a dangerous animal. My choice is a Lyman 48 or 57 peepsight, with the old Redfield gold-faced Sourdough front sight. For night work or any close-range shooting, just screw the aperture out of the rear sight, then put it away and forget about it. All you need is the ghost ring to center the front sight. It is very quick to do and accuracy is not diminished.

I must tell you about a strange series of events that made a particular bait hunt really stand out in my mind. The bear, about a three hundred and fifty-pounder, had killed an old ewe and dragged it to the edge of a hillside covered with lodgepole pine. My blind was about thirty yards from where the ewe had been half-eaten and partially covered. I sat two nights with no results.

On the third night, a friend named Louie wanted to come along with me to the blind. We entered the blind about an hour and a half before dark, just as the shadows were melting into twilight. We had been there forty-five minutes when Louie began to complain that an abscessed tooth was bothering him. Fifteen minutes later he said he didn't think he could spend the night because the pain was growing more severe. Having seen this before, I let him off the hook by advising him to go to the truck and take some aspirin, which I told him was in the glove compartment. He apologized profusely for leaving me alone, then quickly left. I couldn't help smiling as I watched him making his way through the woods. Over the years I had had nine or ten would-be night baiters suddenly have some pressing reason why they couldn't spend the night so close to a bear's dinner.

The night dragged on slowly with only an occasional coyote circling the carcass. By 3 A.M., the half-moon had disappeared behind the tree line, leaving the area barely visible in the dim starlight. Suddenly the normal night sounds diminished. I was sure the bear was near. The monofilament fish line, strung from the carcass to my left wrist, began to jerk in small, short movements. I knew the bear was sniffing and pulling at the carcass before eating it. After ten or twelve minutes, I heard the unmistakable sounds of a bear tearing and eating greedily.

It is wise to wait a few minutes during the feeding process because the bear will not be as wary as it was upon arrival. Let it relax and enjoy the meal. With my left thumb, I switched on the flashlight fastened to the left side of my rifle. The light stabbed into the darkness to reveal the bear standing in a picture-book pose. Both shoulders were in line for a perfect broadside shot. The gold Sourdough sight fastened on the center of the bear's shoulder. I squeezed off the shot, sending a 250-grain .338 Nosler bullet smashing into the bear's near shoulder with a resounding *whop!* As usual, the recoil turned the flashlight off, leaving me in total darkness. I worked the bolt as quickly as possible, then listened. I heard a bawl of pain and the breaking of sticks as the bear fell into a pile of debris. Most of the time a bear will emit a deep sigh or a mournful death rattle as it expires. But this time all hell broke loose!

There were several loud woofs and wails, followed by the crash of two bodies colliding. I could hear jaws snapping and sounds similar to those of a heavyweight boxer hitting a heavy bag. Though the frenzy lasted about three minutes, it seemed like an eternity as I sat there in the darkness. I flicked on my flashlight.

To my astonishment, a large bear was biting and tearing at the carcass of the bear I had shot. The newcomer swung its head toward the light. I instantly placed the rifle sights on the spot where the bear's spine intersected with its shoulder and touched off a shot. I heard the slap of the bullet and then silence. Thirty seconds later, I heard a deep sigh and knew the second bear was dead.

I was astonished at the turn of events but didn't have a ready explanation. I waited out the remaining hours of darkness, my normal practice. It is a dangerous presumption to leave the blind not knowing if all the hairy participants are through for the night.

At dawn what a sight: two gigantic bears dead, one on top the other! I crawled out of my blind with rifle ready and moved over to investigate. What had baffled me in the night became clear in the light of day. The first bear had not been the killer of the carcass. It had simply caught scent of it and, throwing all caution aside, had come in to feast on another bear's prize. Apparently the owner of the kill had been stalking the intruder at the very moment I had switched on my flashlight. Ignoring my shot, the second bear launched its attack on the thief. The fury of its attack was remarkable. The hide of the first bear was torn to shreds. Bite marks and long gashes were all over the first bear's neck and head. I am sure the bear fight would have lasted a long time had the first bear not already been mortally wounded.

Louie showed up forty-five minutes later, saying he'd been awakened from his sleep in the truck by my first shot. Though six hundred yards away, he had still heard the fight and thought I was being mauled. As he had no weapon or flashlight, he wisely decided not to come to my aid. When he heard the second shot and the quiet that followed, he fully expected to find both the bear and me dead at the scene. Louie was elated to see two bears dead and me alive. He thumped me on the back soundly and shook my hand so hard my teeth rattled. We were a couple of really happy guys.

It is hard to beat the moment of truth in bait hunting: when the light of the flashlight cuts through the darkness and the shot rings out. That moment is one of both fear and excitement. I guess it's not really a case of being afraid of things that go bump in the night as it is of being afraid of things that go *woof!*

If you've never been afraid, try night baiting for one of the most powerful and dangerous carnivores on the face of the earth.

Shoot!

What makes bear hunting exciting is the ever-present threat that a large, powerful, unpredictable carnivore—with very sharp teeth—will attack. Bear attacks, however, rarely occur if the hunter shoots accurately with the right rifle and uses the right bullet. But since this is an imperfect world, and with Murphy's Law always in effect, even the best-laid plans can go terribly awry. The bear doesn't always cooperate in giving you that picture-perfect shot, and sometimes it will move just as you squeeze the trigger, resulting in a bad hit. Also, the hunter may not be up to par that day, his reflexes just a little bit slower than usual. And when a bad hit is made, things get sticky.

Black bear and grizzly act similarly when wounded. Both receive into their system a tremendous shot of adrenaline when hit by a bullet. If they are not killed by the first shot, a follow-up shot often has little or no effect if not placed accurately to break down the bear's bone structure. It is absolutely imperative to hit shoulders, spine, or brain if you expect to incapacitate the bear immediately. The bear and the Cape buffalo are the only two animals I know that will attack even when mortally wounded.

Don't let anyone kid you: A charging black bear is pound for pound every bit as hard to stop as a grizzly—maybe more so!

In my experience, the two hardest charges to stop were both made by black bears. It doesn't take much to envision what happens to the hunter if the bear, filled with rage and adrenaline, reaches him with all its fighting equipment still in working order. The following story is about a black bear charge that still sends shivers up my spine when I think about it.

It was early October in the eastern Cascades of Washington State. A few moderate snows had fallen in the higher elevations, and every other day there was rain and sleet. For about a week and a half C. E. Barnett and I had been discussing a big black that had been running berry pickers and elk hunters off the terraces of Sugarloaf Mountain. We had both decided that this particular bear had to be destroyed since it had become a distinct threat to anyone in the area. At the higher elevations, the huckleberries had all dropped, but at the lower ones, where Sugarloaf Mountain was, some bushes still had enough ripe berries to attract bears putting the finishing touches on their winter fat. C. E. and I firmly believed that if we didn't destroy the bear now we would have to do it in the spring.

C. E.'s friend Harold had been pestering C. E. to take him bear hunting. Late one evening C. E. called and said: "Do you mind if we take Harold with us in the morning when we go after that bear we were talking about last week?"

"Do we hafta?" I asked.

"I can't put him off much longer," replied C. E. "He'll think I don't want him to go!"

I laughed to myself and thought what a great guy C. E. is, always thinking of the other fellow. "Sure, bring him along," I told C. E. hesitantly, for my heart was telling me it was a mistake.

At 4 A.M. next morning, C. E. arrived in his little red-and-white Nissan Patrol vehicle. I walked out of the house carrying my rifle and backpack, then opened the passenger door to behold Harold. He was six foot four, about two hundred forty pounds, and was wearing orange from head to toe. I struggled to keep from laughing, wondering why he was decked out in a bright hunting outfit when there wasn't likely to be another person within twenty miles of us on a weekday at that hour of the morning. With my best manners, I said, "Hello, Harold," then added in a tight-lipped way, "Ready to go hunting?" He said he was ready, but I noticed something lacking in his affirmation.

On the drive to the mountain there was the usual chitchat that goes with hunting bears, and to all appearances everyone was having a good time. But tension surfaced when I asked Harold what type of rifle he was using.

"I'm using a new .300 Weatherby," he said, "with 220-grain Barnes bullets."

"Well, that should do the trick," I said.

Harold then launched into a total rundown of the ballistics of that particular bullet and cartridge combination from zero to a thousand yards, which indicated that at least he had done some research on equipment for hunting black bear.

During the drive, C. E. explained that Sugarloaf Mountain was three-quarters of a mile long and about a quarter-mile across, and that the east side of the mountain was naturally terraced. Indeed, there were five terraces thirty-five to forty yards wide on the east side that were covered with unstable talus fragments, making ideal nesting areas for the marmots. C. E. said that bears would be digging for marmots on the slope around 9:30 or 10 A.M. After eating their main course, the bears would switch to huckleberries for dessert. We planned to travel the road running along the third terrace at a slow speed listening for rolling rocks, which would indicate that a bear was on the slope digging for marmots. C. E. told our guest that when we heard rolling rocks we would climb the slope till we saw the feeding bear. C. E. would use his bear-call, which exactly imitated the cries of a marmot badly injured. The bear would cease digging and back out of the hole to investigate, and C. E. would tell Harold when to shoot the bear. Then C. E. launched into a detailed explanation of exactly where to shoot it.

While listening to C. E., Harold's lips were tightly drawn across his face. He was noticeably agitated, and at least five times before reaching our destination, he asked C. E.: "Tell me where I hit him again?" C. E. and I knew his confidence was failing fast, and at that moment we should have declined to take him any farther, but we could not think of a graceful way to do it.

We reached the terrace road on the side of Sugarloaf, rolled our windows down, and proceeded in the Nissan at a two-mile-an-hour crawl. Light was breaking to allow us to see well enough to shoot. We then heard above us the telltale *clunk, clunk, clunk* of rolling talus. C. E. whispered, "There he be, let's go get him." We got out of the car and into the frosty morning air, uncased our rifles, and started picking our way up the slope as quietly as possible. The sun was just hitting the top of the ridge when we arrived at the fifth terrace.

We could clearly see a huge black rump sticking out of the bank at the top of the mountain approximately one hundred twenty-five yards above us. I very carefully stepped ten yards to the left of C. E., keeping a close eye on the bear's every move. The bear was really making a din as it rolled huge rocks between its hind legs, sending them bounding down the slope. C. E. whispered to the hunter, "When I blow he'll pull his head out of the hole and look for the marmot. When I say 'Shoot,' you shoot right through his shoulders. You got it?"

"Yeah," replied Harold, stepping about three paces to C. E.'s left. C. E. blew twice on the call and, sure enough, the bear pulled its head out and looked for the marmot.

"Shoot," whispered C. E.

"Now?" said the hunter.

"Shoot," said C. E., this time with intensity.

"Now?" said the hunter.

Shortly thereafter the bear stuck its head back in the hole and continued digging. C. E., with a perplexed look on his face, said, "That bear's not going to dig forever! When I say 'shoot' you shoot." Harold nodded and C. E. blew mightily again. The bear cooperated perfectly, pulling its body completely out of the hole and turning sideways to give Harold a perfect shot.

"Shoot!" said C. E.

"Now?" said the hunter.

The bear stuck its head back into the hole a second time. My mouth must have been hanging open in utter disbelief! C. E., a very religious man whom I had never heard curse over any situation, said, "Dammit! That bear's going to either get our scent any minute or hear us, and when he does he'll be gone." Harold was licking his lips and his eyes stuck out like buttons. C. E. said sternly, "When I blow this time, you shoot!"

Miraculously, the bear had not heard any of the whispered conversation since it was entirely enthralled in digging out breakfast. But it almost didn't matter. The same scene repeated itself. C. E. blew the whistle, the bear pulled its head out, C. E. said to shoot, and Harold asked, "Now?"

C. E. was really perturbed. "Shoot, dammit!" he said, gritting his teeth. The bear put its head back in the hole.

Then Harold shot!

His aim was good—just a little late—and with a resounding thump the 220-grain Barnes walloped the bear right square in the rump. Contrary to popular belief, bears do not growl but they do roar, which is what this one did. Swinging its upper body out of the hole, it stood on the skyline searching for the cause of its sudden pain and discomfort.

At that moment, all my thoughts of Harold—or of anything else for that matter—totally evaporated. All that occupied me now was one mighty mad bear with eyes focused on C. E., Harold, and me. With unbelievable speed it launched itself into a charge down the slope. Its jaws popped like a .22, and a six-foot-long string of saliva trailed from its mouth. Its lips jutted prominently forward and its ears lay completely out of sight. Yep, this was a real charge! No bluff here!

I heard the report of C. E.'s .300 Weatherby, and over my own sights I could see dust and hair spew from the bear's shoulder as the 180-grain Nosler smashed into bone. The bear's shoulder caved in, causing it to do two somersaults, and then it continued its charge.

The gold sight on my .358-99 Savage lined up on the bear's shoulder as it ran toward us with one leg clearly immobilized. I touched off a shot. The bear rolled and came up again, running on three legs. The sight was really terrible. The bear's saliva was now streaming red, and its roars were interspersed with bawls of pain. I was sure I had hit it and aimed at exactly the same place and fired again. The bullet kicked up dust on the bear's chest near the shoulder socket.

A split second after my shot, C. E. fired a second time. The bear tumbled at least three times before hitting the bottom of the talus slope, regained its feet, and was now thirty-five yards away and coming straight at us. C. E.'s rifle boomed a third time. The bear went down on its belly, regained its feet, and started ripping four-foot-long strings of intestines out of the exit wound. Blood sprayed like a yard sprinkler as the bear shook its head left and right.

It was twenty yards away when I realized I needed to adjust my aim. I had been shooting just inside the shoulder socket. I now aimed about an inch and a half farther to the left and touched off the last shot I was capable of firing before the bear reached us. The shot was good and I could see fur and dust fly off its shoulder. The bear slammed forward on its belly, its front legs trailing helplessly beside its body. It slowly pushed itself through the shintangle with its hind legs till it was five yards from me. It was still full of fight—dead—but not knowing it.

I aimed very carefully my .44 Magnum, for now there was no immediate hurry, and put a bullet into its brain, ending the most furious and determined charge I had ever witnessed.

I heard C. E. say, "I've gotta sit down!"

I felt the same way, but as I moved toward a resting spot I almost tripped over Harold's .300 Weatherby lying on the shintangle. Harold! I had completely forgotten about him! I took several quick steps to the edge of the slope and looked down the slide. There he was, one hundred fifty yards away, running at full speed and leaping brush like a deer.

"By golly, that guy surely can jump," said C. E., as we watched him disappear from view. "Hope he don't kill himself."

Since we couldn't catch Harold, we turned to the carcass. All three of C. E.'s shots had entered the bear's left side and exited at the right hip. His first bullet had broken the left shoulder, and his follow-up shots hit so close to that of the first that very little new internal damage resulted. My first two hits had missed the right shoulder socket by an inch and a half, which left the bear mobile on three legs but caused a lot of internal damage. My third shot hit squarely on the ball socket, breaking its right shoulder to finally drop it.

"I think if either one of us had been alone," said C. E., "we would have gotten chewed by that bear!"

I concurred wholeheartedly. There are times when its great to have a partner you can count on!

After skinning the bear and placing the hide on my packboard, I shouldered the load and started down the hill with C. E., who carried the three rifles. We unloaded the bear hide into the Nissan, then set out to find Harold. We followed his tracks to the creek below, helped by shreds of orange fabric clinging to the oak and willow branches along the way. Neither of us said anything, but we were both hoping Harold hadn't hurt himself seriously on his pell-mell descent.

We found Harold sitting by the creek, elbows on knees, head in hands, sobbing in humiliation. Not a shred of orange remained on his body, which was a mass of scrapes and scratches. Adding to his sad state, we could tell with a glance and a couple of whiffs that he had urinated and defecated at some time during the ordeal. We would have laughed but we felt too sorry for him. We tried to console him but to no avail, though we did manage to get him to take a bath in the creek. We had brought spare clothes with us from the Nissan, anticipating that we might need them.

Harold was disconsolate during our return trip. Though I never saw him again, I still feel sad that he had to experience the ultimate embarrassment for a bear hunter—running from a charge.

While old Harold's flight may seem humorous to the reader, don't be too quick to condemn him until you've experienced furry fury bearing down on you! What happened to Harold wasn't the first time someone lost control in the face of a bear charge, and it won't be the last.

Remember, when a giant bear is wounded by a poorly placed shot, nothing—*nothing*—will stop it but a properly constructed bullet placed in the brain, spine, or shoulders by a cool, steady marksman with an adequate rifle. You can't outrun a bear!

By the way, the bear was the second largest C. E. and I had ever killed. It weighed about five hundred pounds and, when stretched out, was a little less than eight feet long.

And to give this story a happy ending, C. E. wrote me later that he and Harold had gone hunting several times after that incident and on one hunt Harold had been charged and reacted nobly, thereby acquitting himself.

Surprise!

My two vocations were law enforcement officer and predator controller. Certainly both jobs involved hunting–one of men and one of animals. Many times I told police officers under my command that the most dangerous situations they will ever encounter are those that occur from a state of total surprise. It is my firm belief that if an officer is well trained and equipped, as well as mentally aware, he can cope with almost any situation. The real danger comes when his mind is not concentrated. The same is true of the hunter who fails to stay alert even in the most tranquil setting. Being in bear country is exactly the same as being in an urban environment. There are critters in both locales that can kill you. It is necessary to be in a state of relaxed alertness in both environments. The following two tales are about my own level of concentration in bear country. Both stories could have had tragic endings.

Back in the 1950s a friend of mine, Howard Lupton, who was living in northwest Wyoming near the border of Yellowstone National Park, had been having real difficulties with a five-hundred-pound boar grizzly that routinely visited his ranch to steal a beef dinner. The bear sauntered over from the park two or three times a month to pick off a young calf or half-grown steer. This had been going on for three years. Both state and federal wildlife trappers and the park personnel had tried to deal with this offender but had had absolutely no success bringing it to bay.

It was in early May 1954, while I was visiting my friend, that the grizzly started its fourth year of depredation. The night after my arrival the silvertip killed a seven-hundred-pound steer, eating a sizable portion and then covering the carcass to return to it later.

Howard and I wanted to devise a plan that we hoped would lead to the demise of the bear we had come to know as "Mr. Hershey," because of its chocolate coat. Using a full frontal attack, which is the killing style of the grizzly, it had snapped the steer's neck by reaching over the animal's boss and fastening its teeth at the back of the neck, then twisting furiously. The bear opened the steer between the steer's hind legs and worked upward into the steer's chest cavity to dine on particular delicacies. We could tell by the drag marks that it had moved the steer—pulling for over two hundred yards an animal roughly two hundred pounds over its own weight. Old Griz then very carefully covered what was left with sticks, small limbs, grass, and sod, making for a sizable burial mound at the edge of the pasture.

Up to this point it looked like an easy proposition. The carcass was located at the corner of a hay meadow with heavy brush all around. Envision a right angle formed by the meadow fence, with a wash about six to seven feet deep bisecting the angle northeast to southwest. The wash ran into the forest near the cornerpost. The prevailing winds in the valley usually blew from the south-southwest. When I approached the carcass along the fence line from the northwest, the wind came from my right, blowing my scent away from the bear if it lay in the woods just outside the fence line. This would make it relatively easy to approach the carcass early in the morning or late in the evening. I checked the burial mound four days straight, morning and evening. The bear had not returned. I knew, though, and with absolute certainty, that it would return within the week.

Saturday was the fifth day after the kill, and, like all cowboys, Howard and I decided to go to town Saturday night. Instead of making the usual 6 P.M. check of the mound, I checked it at 3 P.M. to enable me to get home in time to make the trip into town. It was a warm, balmy afternoon with the sun shining brightly and about a three-mile-an-hour breeze blowing directly from the west. As I approached the fence line, I could clearly see the mound from one hundred yards away. I glanced casually at the mound, and it looked undisturbed. Though I knew never to approach a bear's food cache without caution, I was more relaxed than I should have been.

I was carrying a Model 70 Winchester in .300 loaded with 220-grain Barnes bullets. It was cradled in the crook of my left arm, my finger was inside the trigger guard, and my thumb rested against the safety. I had approached to within thirty-five yards of the mound when I noticed something wrong. Terribly wrong. A fresh drag mark circled from the back of the mound to the wash, which slanted away to my left. I felt the hair on my neck stand straight up and a chill run up my spine. I realized instantly the danger I was in.

I never heard a sound, but an inner warning mechanism told me to do a 90-degree pivot. The grizzly was charging, lips extended and ears back. With only ten yards between us, I had no time to raise the rifle, so I pointed it level, snaked off the safety, and fired. The bear rolled one somersault and came to rest with its head about three feet from my left foot. Blood trickled from the bullet hole on the inside corner of its left eye. Though I felt instinctively that it was over, I worked the bolt and fired another round into the top of the silvertip's head. Its legs extended and went rigid. The body shuddered in convulsion and relaxed.

My legs couldn't carry me any longer. I sat down cross-legged facing the bear, remaining completely still for at least ten minutes. I had almost made a fatal error—assuming too much and seeing too little. What still astounds me is how quietly the bear had charged. No woof, no snap of its jaws—it was as absolutely silent as a five-hundred-pound ghost!

The bear had opened the backside of the burial mound and dragged the carcass forty-five yards up the streambed. The breeze had notified it of my presence at almost exactly the same time I had discovered my near fatal error. If it had not been for my maintaining a slender thread of caution, I would have been its next victim! Remember—never take anything for granted when in the proximity of a bear!

Another close call occurred only eight years ago. The difference this time was that I was far older and more experienced.

It occurred in late May. I was on the northwest end of Black Mountain near Craig, Colorado, where there is a large basin formed by Sand Point on the west, Mount Oliphant on the south, and Mount Welba on the east. I was scouting for a place suitable for baiting a large black bear that called this basin its home. I started off that morning from Stan and Janette McAnally's place, which borders the Routt National Forest. The McAnallys, who are friends of mine, own property in the Wilderness Ranch housing addition on Black Mountain. I have used their mountain home as the starting point for many bear and elk hunts.

This particular morning didn't seem much different than many others that I had spent looking for spring baiting grounds. The only exception was that there was more snow on the ground than usual this late in May. Ordinarily my bait would have been in place two weeks earlier, but the extra snow had delayed me.

There is a beautiful little stream that runs directly behind McAnally's cabin that I usually followed to reach two meadows, about a half-mile apart and connected by an old logging trail. The grade of the trail increases rapidly, and along it there is a mixture of spruce and lodgepole pine, which limit shooting distances to only ten to fifty yards. The snow was melting rapidly at the spots where sunrays penetrated the forest canopy. The shadowed areas were still covered with fifteen to twenty inches of crusted snow, making silent walking nearly impossible on parts of the trail.

Since I was not really hunting, I was carrying the lightest rifle I own, a sporterized .303 Enfield (Jungle Carbine) with iron sights. As I approached the second meadow, heavy woods hugged the trail's left side. The sun had melted most of the snow on this part of the trail, so I walked along very quietly.

Ten yards ahead, the trail made a sharp left turn. I stopped, and for some unaccountable reason I felt a reluctance to make the turn. I put the rifle in the high-ready position, flipped off the safety, and took up the slack on the military-style trigger. At that moment I heard a soft *woof,* and a large shape materialized out of the dark forest at the turn in the trail. It was a five-hundred-pound grizzly ten yards away with its ears waving back and forth and its nose wiggling. It was trying its best to figure out what I was. I'm sure it never heard me until it heard the click of the safety.

We stood facing each other for what seemed like ten minutes but was probably more like ten seconds. Finally, my scent drifted to its nostrils and I could clearly see the guard hairs on its neck and shoulders rise. The grizzly's ears swiveled back out of sight and then flipped forward again. It was having trouble making up its mind whether to charge or run. Then its ears drew back and stayed, and its head slowly lowered about three to four inches. It was considering very seriously an all-out charge.

Trying to keep my voice as low pitched as possible under the circumstances, I began to talk to the bear in what I hoped was a quiet, well-modulated tone. I could see its indecision reasserting itself. The animal's ears once again swung forward and its head raised to its original position. I said something like "Well, old boy, I sure didn't intend to make you mad. Just take it easy while I walk out of here." I stepped to the right, a neutral area, because I didn't want to give the impression of retreating or advancing—either of which might have been an indication of fear or aggression. I saw the bear visibly relax, the hair on its neck lowering. It now seemed more curious than angry. It walked toward me three steps to get a better view with clearly no aggression intended. I moved fifteen yards into the timber and circled the bear's position until I felt I could once again safely resume the trail.

I never saw the bear again because I went back to McAnally's cabin by another route. The next week I traveled the same trail and discovered that the grizzly had finished the remains of a winterkilled elk calf. The scene clearly showed me what had transpired. The grizzly, probably about a month or so out of hibernation and much in need of protein, had found the elk and proceeded to dine on it. After its long sleep, its stomach was not yet accustomed to digesting full-sized feeds. What it normally would have cleaned up in two or three days took a week to finish. The grizzly probably had been asleep by the carcass when I approached. A combination of my "sixth sense" and the click of my safety probably prevented an encounter in which one or both of us might have died. If I had turned that corner and the bear had awoken to see a human that close to its prize, there undoubtedly would have been instant retaliation.

I hope these two incidents will help keep you alert in bear country. It is not that there is a bear behind every tree, but there may be a bear behind a tree you someday pass. Be alert and stay ready! I know what the experts say: "There are no more grizzly bears in Colorado." But regardless of what organizations like the Division of Wildlife maintain, I have seen seven grizzlies in Colorado with positive ID since 1959. Where the bear in this story came from I am reluctant to even hazard a guess, but it may have been a visitor from Wyoming. Just passing through, perhaps.

Bear Bluff

I have told you in graphic detail of some of the bear charges
I have experienced. But for every real charge, there may be as
many as thirty bluff charges. It would be beneficial if we could
always tell exactly what the bear had in mind when it launched
its charge, but unfortunately this is impossible. In time, however,
one can distinguish a bluff charge from the real thing 95 percent
of the time. The bear tips its paw to what it's really up to.

I often see full-sized bear mounts in the dramatic poses so
loved by writers, artists, and Hollywood filmmakers. The lips
of the mounted bear are set in a curled snarl, like that of a dog,
and its ears are erect. Neither of these characteristics, however,
actually occurs when a bear charges. When preparing to charge,
the bear's head is low and its ears back, its lips protrude, and it
will often be making very little noise unless it is wounded. The
ears are rolled back so that they are not damaged by fang or
claw, and its lips protrude and flare out slightly on the sides so it
can bare its teeth for action.

We must also understand what the bear does when it reaches
its prey. The bear uses its teeth as its primary weapon to inflict a
killing bite. The proverbial "bear hug" almost never occurs except
on rare occasions when the prey is pulled to the bear's chest to

better facilitate a bite to its neck or head. Though its claws are formidable weapons, and many animals have been killed by a bear's powerful blow, they are used mainly for defense from other bears or another animal big and fierce enough to press an attack. I have witnessed bears torn to shreds by massive blows from the defending bear's claws, and I once saw a Hereford bull with the frontal plate of its skull driven back a full inch and a half by the blow from a four-hundred-pound black. Imagine that blow hitting a hundred-and-seventy-five-pound human. Not a pretty thought.

It is important to know that a bear attacks with its teeth, breaking the neck or piercing the skull of its victim with a powerful bite. Occasionally, the bear will choke its prey by biting hard enough to collapse its prey's windpipe, a method similar to that of the African lion.

If you surprise a bear lying asleep beside a trail, it might quite literally "knock your block off" with one swipe of its paw. But the bear is not charging. Many people have been confronted by bears and, to their dying day, honestly believed they were the victims of a charge.

I watched a television program recently in which a fisherman shot a video of what he thought was a black bear charge. While it was excellent footage of a bear at very close range, the bear did not at any time during the entire episode charge; instead, it walked calmly toward the fisherman with its ears erect and tipped forward and its lips in normal position. The bear did not even woof or snap its jaws. Once, it even partially climbed a tree to get a better look at this human interloper. The bear backed the man into the water and calmly looked him over while the man shouted at the bear to leave.

I believe the fisherman thought he was in mortal peril, and I certainly don't blame him for being nearly scared out of his wits. But the truth behind the scenario is this. The man was fishing on a wilderness lake in Ontario, Canada, a place where humans are few and far between. The bear was intensely interested in this biped carrying an eye that whirred. I think it was simply overwhelmed by curiosity. If the bear had meant to harm the fisherman, its ears would have been back and its teeth exposed. In one terrible second, its jaws would have clamped on the man's face at the temples till all struggling ceased.

That is not to say that a curious bear cannot be dangerous in the same way that a curious elk or deer can be if surprised or struck by a blow at close range. If the fisherman had hit the bear's snout with his camera case, the bear might have run off since the man was only an object of curiosity and not of food or anger. On the other hand, the bear might have suddenly changed from a curious investigator into a defensive buzz saw, ending the encounter with fatal results.

I've experienced so many bluff charges that it is almost anticlimactic to see a real charge in progress because the bluff is a lot more entertaining. When a bear bluffs, it will run at you snapping its jaws and woofing. Its hair is erect all the way down its back, and it charges as though it really means business. But the telltale clues that the charge is a bluff are the erect ears, high-head position, and absence of protruding lips. Moreover, the bluffing bear will run full speed to within five yards, put on its brakes, and stand there trying to intimidate. If you stand your ground, you will have done better than most, unless, of course, you couldn't move because you were so terrified. In any case, you did the right thing because to run from a bluff may manifest the bear's predatory instincts, causing the bluff charge to become the real thing.

Remember, do not run from a bear! You will always lose if the bear is within thirty yards. You cannot climb a tree as quickly as a bear can cover thirty yards.

While visiting a gun show in Palmer, Alaska, in spring 1993, I was talking to several brown bear guides when we overheard two young men talking about how fast they could cover ground and scamper up trees. One said all he needed was twenty yards of bare ground between him and the bear to get away safely. I could keep quiet no longer and gently told the young sprinter that he would lose a large chunk of his lower anatomy if he tried that stunt. The young man promptly told me that bears can't run very fast. I asked him how he knew. He said that he'd seen a grizzly bear chase the father in the movie *The Wilderness Family* and that that bear was really slow.

This is the attitude of many people whose only contact with a bear is from a Hollywood film that has little or no resemblance to reality. The other two hunters came to my aid and explained, not quite as delicately as I, that you have no chance escaping a bear serious about catching you.

How fast can a bear run? Some biologists have said the animal can run up to twenty-seven miles per hour over short distances. I have personally clocked a long, lean black bear running flat out on a logging road at forty-three miles per hour over a distance of a hundred fifty yards. Simply put, a bear can cover a hundred yards in four to five seconds and fifty yards in about two and a half to three seconds. So if you intend to outrun one of these boys, you'd better be jet propelled and have on your best pair of Nike's!

The following tale is about a bear encounter that seemed to be both charge *and* bluff. In fall 1992, Jan Roth, a taxidermist, and I were hunting in an area known as Indian Run, southeast of Craig, Colorado. Jan had taken the ridge to my left, carrying his recurved bow and looking for elk while I stayed on the main ridge glassing for bear in the canyon below. Finding cover scant on the ridge, Jan crossed the canyon and moved to a position higher up on the hillside. The area was covered with service and oak brush with occasional spruce and aspen mixed in at the higher elevations.

I decided I would try using a predator call, which sometimes is very effective in luring a bear into rifle range. This type of hunting is totally different from bait hunting. For example, a bear will come in to bait cautiously but it will not be flushed with adrenaline. It will usually come in at a walk, look the situation over, and begin to feed. Just the opposite occurs when you are using predator calls. The bear will usually come running with mouth watering in anticipation of chomping down on some tasty morsel. Its adrenaline level will be high, and you must shoot quickly and accurately if you don't want to have a hungry bear in your lap!

At 10 A.M. I blew my call for the first time. I could hear oak branches snapping at least two hundred yards up the hill. The bear express was on its way. I was standing in the middle of an open area shaped like an 8, with the top circle about ten yards across and the bottom circle about twelve. The bear would be breaking into the top circle of the 8. I raised my rifle to shoulder height, slipped off the safety, and waited.

It wasn't long until a two-hundred-pound black bear skidded to a stop just across the clearing in apparent confusion. Its head was swinging back and forth and it shifted its weight from side to side, much like a cow pony cutting out a calf. I could see the bear was disappointed at not finding the injured fawn, but this did not completely account for its unusual behavior. Upon finding a man in their path, most black bears immediately turn back into the brush or forest. This one didn't! It stood its ground! I could also see the situation was getting worse, for its ears began to rotate from the erect to the flattened position, and it started jerking spasmodically and snapping its jaws like a semiautomatic .22 repeater.

I had the sights on it but didn't pull the trigger, feeling something was strangely amiss. I decided to hold my fire as long as I could, which turned out to be fifteen long seconds. Suddenly, a forty-pound ball of fur brushed my left leg as it rocketed by, followed by another about the same size. Two bear cubs reunited with their mother, joyously putting out their paws to touch the sow's body and face. The sow calmed down and with great dignity strolled off into the dense oak underbrush with the cubs by its side.

I was glad to have had enough experience to determine that this bear had something else on its mind besides eating. The bear charged down the hill at a terrific pace, and the cubs had gotten lost trying to keep up with Mom and had inadvertently come out into the clearing (the bottom circle of the 8) directly behind me. Jan said he had heard the bear snort as it took off down the hill but was unable to guess the outcome. The bear was, of course, alarmed at having a man between it and its cubs. Not seeing the cubs, I was totally at a loss trying to determine what was causing the bear such great anxiety. Luckily, though, I was able to tell immediately that this was an unusual situation, thereby avoiding a woodland tragedy. It was neither a charge nor a bluff. It was, to be sure, a difficult situation to make sense of, but at least it had a happy ending. Jan didn't take home an elk and I didn't take home a bear, but I did take home a great memory that I will never forget.

Tunnel of Death

C. E. Barnett and I were looking for a small sheep-killing bear on the Yakima Indian Reservation at the upper Abtahum Ridge in Washington State. C. E. had been hunting this particular bruin for about two weeks with no luck whatsoever. We knew it was a female and probably five or six years old. Its fur was light cinnamon brown and it weighed about one hundred eighty-five pounds.

What distinguished these attacks from others was how savage they were. The bear would run full speed into a group of sheep, knocking them over like bowling pins as it snapped its jaws and swung its paws right and left. Its pell-mell attacks would usually seriously injure six or seven sheep in addition to the one it picked to eat. We knew the bear would be a particularly nasty customer from its general display of a bad attitude. We had tried baits, only to find that this was one of the few bears we had encountered that refused to come back even once to a kill. It preferred fresh prey every day. We were operating under extreme pressure from the sheepherders and the tribal counsel to end this predatory threat. Consequently, we decided to put out five or six snares in the immediate area even though we didn't like to hunt this way. Using snares meant we would sometimes catch the wrong bear and then have to go through the lengthy process of tranquilizing the innocent critter, releasing it, and resetting the snare. We'd already caught four innocent bears, losing five days in the process.

It was July 2nd. I remember the day clearly because I had told C. E. my services as a police officer were needed for the Fourth of July celebration at Toppenish, Washington. After today, I told C. E., I would not be available to assist him for another few days.

By 10 A.M. that day it was 84 degrees, warmer than usual at the elevation at which we were working. To check four snares on the upper end of the ridge, we had to walk four miles and consequently had worked up a healthy sweat. I suggested to C. E. that we should take a break and drink some water. We sat down on a flat rock and looked out at the valley. Five minutes later our unbelieving eyes saw the cinnamon bear, walking along in broad daylight without a care in the world!

Since it was the middle of the day and neither of us had expected to see a bear on a midday stroll, we were caught unprepared. I had not brought my rifle and C. E. was carrying his little .243 Sako Sporter. The only other weapon between us was my four-inch Model 29 S&W .44 Magnum, stoked with 250-grain Keith bullets and 22 grains of 2400 powder.

I asked him what bullet he was using and he said it was a 105-grain Speer. I felt waves of doubt as I realized that the shot he would have to take was downhill at a target three hundred twenty yards distant. I looked at C. E. and could tell he was thinking the same thing. "That's a whale of a long shot," he muttered.

C. E. hunched into a tight-sitting position, sighted through the four-power Leupold, and touched off a well-aimed shot. Watching through my 7X50 binoculars, I saw the dust and hair erupt from the bear's neck just in front of the shoulder. It dropped without a twitch and we started walking down to what we thought was a dead bear. A slight hummock about thirty yards from the bear temporarily hid the animal from view. Upon cresting the hill we saw absolutely nothing—no bear in sight! We both jerked to attention, with C. E. taking the rifle to his shoulder and me grabbing my .44.

Realizing this could be a sticky situation, we separated ten yards and advanced slowly to where the bear had lain. C. E. suggested that he look for the bear and I look for its blood trail. I could see small splatters of deep red blood, indicating that the shot might have missed the artery and had been only a flesh wound. C. E. and I started getting nervous after covering about two hundred fifty yards of brush-covered ground and finding no bear. We stopped for a breather and took stock of the situation.

"I'm afraid I know where that bear's headed," said C. E. I knew the country about as well as he and knew also where the bear was headed: to a windfall (a place where trees had been knocked down by a mighty wind), which was about four hundred fifty yards long and one hundred fifty yards wide. If the bear had crawled into that mass of logs, we would have a devil of a time getting it out.

By the time we arrived at the windfall, the blood trail had almost disappeared, indicating that the wound was sealing itself with either hide slippage or coagulating blood. What remained, however, led us straight to a bear tunnel.

"What do you think?" asked C. E.

"Well, I won't be able to come back tomorrow," I said. "We'll have to do what we're going to do today." We sat there another ten minutes, contemplating the horror of what had to be done.

C. E. broke the silence. "Who's gonna do it, you or me?"

With the brashness of youth, I said, "I guess I'll do it."

"I'll be back before four," said C. E., handing me the rifle. "I'm going to the truck to get the flashlight." C. E. left at a mountain man's trot.

Alone now, I began to reconsider my volunteering to do something so dangerous, and I decided I would go through with it only when I saw C. E. returning with the five-cell flashlight. I kneeled down and peered into the bear tunnel, seeing a small circle of light at its end. C. E. went to look for a blood trail leading out of the tunnel but could not find one. He yelled to me, "No such luck—she's still in there. I'll shoot her if she comes out this end." You might question our speaking loudly at a time

like this, but since we had been there for over two hours, we knew the bear knew we were there and that it was waiting patiently for us to make the first move.

The big problem I now faced was that I didn't know how many side tunnels intersected with the one I was preparing to crawl into. I proceeded four yards into the tunnel and examined the tightly packed and interlaced trunks, limbs, and needles for any sign of hidden alcoves or connecting tunnels. After thirty yards, my "sixth sense" asserted itself. I could feel the hair stand on my neck and a slight chill run along my spine. Knowing a wild beast was in there that could easily tear me apart, I felt the compelling urge to get out.

I said a short prayer because I suddenly felt totally incapable of pulling this one off and emerging in one piece. I swallowed hard and waited a moment for God to intervene. Just then, I heard a *woof* directly in front. I began to inch forward—and I do mean inch! As I played the flashlight along the left wall of the tunnel, I saw a shadowy spot that looked like a depression. I rolled to my right side with my back hard-pressed against the wall and extended my right arm, a cocked pistol in hand. To steady myself, I pressed the back of my right hand against the back of my left hand, which held the flashlight. Slowly I pushed forward with my legs. I could see the black tip of a nose come into view. *Just a little bit more and I could get off a killing shot,* I thought. *Please wait, bear, just a second longer!* I dug my toes in and pushed forward six inches.

I clearly saw the bear's face, and I could tell instantly that it was lying flat on its tummy with its head propped on its forepaws, waiting like a cat for a mouse. Its nose was tipped up slightly, and I knew if I placed the bullet right on it the bullet would travel up the nasal canal and straight into the brain. I could see the bear's unblinking eyes and knew it wouldn't wait much longer. It was now or never. I centered the red insert front sight on the end of its nose and squeezed the trigger.

BOOM! The recoil extinguished the flashlight! The muzzle blast blew up a large cloud of dust from the four-inch-deep powder on the tunnel floor, choking and blinding me! I expected any second to be turned into a shredded rug!

"Are you OK?! Are you OK?!" shouted C. E.

"I'm OK–I think," I managed to say between coughs. Gradually the dust cloud settled, but my ears were still ringing from the shot. I ventured to turn on the flashlight. Through the murky haze I could see the bear lying exactly as it had been but with a trickle of blood now running from a black hole at the end of its snout. The bear was dead.

It was almost dark by the time I got out of the tunnel. C. E. said he would bring several Indians with him tomorrow to help drag the bear out. This turned out to be an impossible chore, however, so he skinned it in the tunnel while lying on his side.

As best he could in such cramped quarters, C. E. examined the carcass and found two interesting facts pertaining to why the bear had such a mean disposition. In its nose he found large porcupine quills driven completely through the top palate of the mouth. Quills were also sticking through the bear's chin and into the tongue, creating a mass of infected tissue. It's hard to imagine the agony that bear must have gone through before my bullet mercifully ended its suffering. C. E.'s bullet had gone through the base of the bear's neck, barely clipping the top of the vertebra. That was why the bear went down instantly but did not stay down.

I will tell you this with absolute certainty: I will never again crawl into such a restricted passage after a wounded bear. I cannot adequately describe the coppery taste in my mouth, the cold feet, the sweaty palms, and the wave of panic that rolled through me that warm summer day in the tunnel of death!

Keith and the Three Bears

Some of you are probably familiar with the name of the noted hunter, marksman, guide, and author Elmer Keith. I have shared many interesting adventures with Elmer Keith, but if you think this chapter is about him, you are mistaken. The "Keith" in the chapter's title refers to my son, Keith Carr. Keith has always been one of my biggest fans and has brightened many days by asking me to tell a bear story. Well, Keith, here are three bear stories that are really about you!

In the summer of 1970 my family and I were living in Albuquerque, New Mexico. My wife, Anne, took Keith and our daughter, Carolyn, to the El Porvenir Christian Camp near Las Vegas, New Mexico. The camp is located in rugged mountain terrain ideally suited for bears, which brings me to the story of my boy's first bear hunt.

At the time, I was working for the Bernalillo County Sheriffs' Office and had a rare Saturday night off. Early Saturday morning my family and I drove to the Christian camp to spend the day. Upon our arrival I learned from A. B. Martinez, the year-round camp caretaker, that a sow bear had been visiting the camp every night for the past week. A. B. was concerned that sooner or later the bear would become a danger to the campers and staff members. The bear had not yet shown aggression, but A. B. was still hoping I could do something about the animal. He had already received written permission from the local officer of the Division of Wildlife to destroy it.

I couldn't pass up A. B.'s offer and asked if he had a rifle I could use. He went to his house and brought back an old Winchester .30-30 "SaddleRing" Carbine. I looked it over. It was in fine mechanical condition even though virtually all its blued finish had been worn off. Knowing A. B. was a pretty fair shot and that we had shot each other's firearms, I trusted his recommendation and took the little rifle bear hunting.

Keith, eight years old at the time, stood listening to the conversation with eyes big as saucers. As soon as he could get a word in he said, "Dad, can I go with you? Can I?"

There would be very little real danger in bringing him since the hunt would occur in daylight and in fairly open juniper and pine terrain. "Let's go see what Mom says," I told him. Anne agreed to let him go but with the proviso that I keep a close eye on him and not track a wounded bear with him present. Since the bear had not been wounded or shown aggressive behavior, I was not expecting any trouble and intended to kill it cleanly with one shot.

We had hunted about two hours and had followed the bear's trail about a mile and a half over some pretty rugged ground. Keith was really warming to the hunt. With youthful exuberance, he walked three yards ahead, doing his best to track the bear. When we came to a possible ambush sight, I would take the lead just in case. We were both having a good time, but I was also getting a little nervous because he kept getting too far ahead. I decided that if he got ten yards ahead without heeding my admonitions, I would have to teach him a lesson.

Sure enough, Keith exceeded the maximum safety distance and without a word I stepped off the trail behind a fairly large ponderosa pine. Peeking between a bush and the pine, I watched my boy amble along looking hard at the trail for bear tracks. He went about another five yards and looked back. Not seeing me, he froze with a look of uncertainty on his face.

"Dad?" he said very quietly.

I didn't answer.

"Dad?" he said again, his voice trembling.

I still didn't answer.

He grimaced in terror and screamed at the top of his lungs: "Dad! Dad! Where are you?!"

Seeing that the lesson had gone too far, I stepped from behind the tree and said, "Here I am, Son."

Tears gushing, he ran over and threw his arms around me for dear life. If he had only known how utterly ashamed I was for scaring him so badly. We hugged each other tightly for a few minutes, and during those minutes something passed between father and son, something that might be called magic. It was a moment I'll never forget.

Only two weeks ago I was talking to Keith and asked if he remembered his first bear hunt. He said, "I sure do. We didn't get the bear."

"Anything else?" I asked.

"Yeah. I learned a lesson from my dad not to get too far ahead and not to get separated—especially in bear country!"

"That sure was a dirty trick I played on you," I said, "and I really felt ashamed for scaring you so badly."

"Well, look at it this way, Pop," Keith replied. "It must have been worth it because I never did that again."

Come to think of it, he never did!

* * * * * *

In fall 1972 I was working in New Mexico as town marshal of Red River, which is nestled high in the mountains between Questa and Eagle Nest. The year in Red River was broken up into seasonal highs and lows based on tourism: summer tourist season, fall lull before winter ski season; winter ski season, spring lull before summer tourist season. During spring and fall lulls, I was occasionally able to spend evenings with my family, which was impossible during the tourist seasons because I would have to be on patrol almost every evening. The ten o' clock news had just come on when my part-Labrador retriever/part-German shepherd, Sarge, started doing his best intruder bark.

My neighbors were on vacation, and I thought it would be very funny if I caught some simple-minded burglar burglarizing the house right next to the town marshal's. I grabbed my Colt .357, slipped out the door, and headed through the darkness to my neighbor's house, which is located on a ten-foot hill. I walked up the hill, dropped to one knee, and peered into the blackness. Once my eyes adjusted I saw a large form standing near the back door. It was a thief all right, though of a different type—a four-hundred-fifty-pound black bear known to Red River residents as "Big Bottom Blackie."

I had just made the positive ID of the offender when a voice directly behind me said, "It's a bear!" I nearly jumped out of my boots! Keith had quietly slipped out of the house and followed me!

I had been hunting Blackie for two seasons now and had never laid eyes on it when I had a weapon. *Well, it is bear season,* I thought. *I've got a license in my pocket and a .357 in my hand.* Then I thought: *The .357 is really not much of a bear gun even in the hands of an experienced shooter, and I've got my son standing right behind me.*

I leaned to Keith and whispered, "Go get your .30-30 and be very quiet about it."

The bear was trying to get into my neighbor's back porch through the screen door. With Sarge raising such a ruckus, it hadn't even heard me, nor had it scented me. All of a sudden a tremendous commotion took place as Keith, running back to the house, jammed his foot in Sarge's water bucket. The bucket stuck tight, clanking with every step and creating so much noise that Sarge stopped barking to see what had happened. Keith finally made it to the house, and Blackie, its attention diverted, dropped to all fours and faced me five yards distant.

Several anxious minutes passed while the bear tried to decide whether to fight or run; then it wheeled and went the other way as fast as its four legs could carry it. Keith, huffing and puffing, arrived with the rifle and shoved it into my extended hand. Blackie had gone forty yards when it stopped and looked back. I looked over the sights but it was too dark to deliver a properly placed hit. I took the rifle off my shoulder and watched the bear walk sedately into the darkness.

"I'm sorry, Dad," said Keith. "I really messed up, didn't I?"

"Yeah, I guess you could say that."

I think he could tell I wasn't all that angry. When we got back in the house, I told Anne and Carolyn about our adventure. They had been watching but couldn't really tell what had happened.

I gave Keith a stern reprimand for following me outside on a possible burglary in progress, explaining how dangerous it could have been. By the end of my reprimand he looked miserable, so I smiled, causing his face to brighten.

"Dad, you mean I'm not gonna get a spanking?" he said.

"No," I said. "But you might if you keep putting your feet in water buckets when I send you after a rifle."

By now the whole situation had become thoroughly amusing and I began to laugh. Seeing he was off the hook, Keith began to laugh too, though more from relief than from realizing the comedy of the episode. Many times over the years Keith and I have shared a laugh when remembering that night.

* * * * * *

My third tale occurred when Keith was thirteen years old. Bear came regularly to the Red River city dump, and Keith and I had decided to go to the dump one evening to observe the bears having supper. We walked a trail that ran along a hillside and headed to the east end of the landfill. The hillside dropped sharply for about one hundred thirty yards to the dumpsite. The main ridge of the hill curved up in a northwesterly direction, creating a bowl-like depression at the north end of the dump. Our location seemed like the perfect place from which to watch foraging bears.

About forty-five minutes before dark, a one-hundred-thirty-pound cinnamon bear arrived and began to nose through the garbage, followed by a medium-sized black female with two black cubs and one brown one. The cinnamon bear gave the mother and cubs a lot of room, so the sow tolerated the young cinnamon. They had been eating for about fifteen minutes when I heard rocks rolling off the rim on the north side of the bowl. We couldn't see the bear because it came off the rise, but we could sure hear its progress! The bear came down the hillside with reckless indifference to the commotion it was causing. We listened for almost ten minutes, following its progress around the southeast rim. I felt we were very lucky that it was making a lot of noise because, since we were on the trail it was coming in on, we could prepare ourselves for its arrival. Given the racket it was making, I knew it was a male. A big male!

Five minutes later the bear came into sight about twenty-five yards distant. Since it wasn't hunting season and we hadn't been experiencing bear problems in Red River that year, I hadn't bothered to bring a rifle. My son, who was kneeling beside me and also apparently reading my mind, whispered: "I wish we had a rifle."

The bear, not having seen us, stood looking down at the dump site. It was the fourth largest black bear I had ever seen. Wearing an auburn coat and weighing nearly five hundred pounds, the bear was awesome to behold. It did not take long for the breeze to waft our scent to its constantly twitching nose. Its head pivoted sharply and it looked straight at us. The staring contest seemed to last an eternity. The bear was frozen and so were we. Its head then lowered slightly and its ears began to roll back. The situation was beginning to look a little sticky, and I very slowly raised my hand to the butt of my Colt Single Action .32-20 Peacemaker. Not much of a gun against a bear but better than nothing.

The bear held its position for thirty seconds, then decided against aggression and walked slowly back up the hill. It ascended the trail silently as a ghost, without dislodging so much as one rock. Keith and I watched it depart and then started down the hill toward Red River. We didn't say much as we walked, but we both knew we had shared a great experience.

Keith had learned a lot since his first bear encounter, which, you will recall, had ended with his foot in Sarge's bucket. As I opened the door to the car, Keith stood looking at the .32-20 in my holster. "Dad," he said, "you know that isn't a big enough gun. You need to get a bigger one." Who could argue with that from a very young, but very astute, hunter. The next time we went to the dump I was packing a Smith & Wesson .44 Magnum!

Red River

Rampage

The trouble started in mid-September at 11 A.M. A family had rented a cabin in the upper valley outside of town. The cabin was part of a complex comprised of six or seven cabins and a main lodge. The family's cabin was out of sight of the main lodge and about twenty yards from the bank of Red River. The other cabins had already been vacated by the end of August, leaving this family quite alone in the area.

During summer several bears had become regular panhandlers at the complex. On this day at 1 P.M., a three-hundred-sixty-pound brown sow came looking for handouts. The family tried to shoo the bear away but it was persistent, walking in circles thirty or forty yards in front of their door. As the afternoon progressed, it became more and more belligerent. Finally, the father grew tired of the game and threw a rock that smacked the bear on the backside. The bear took off in high gear into the willows along the riverbank. The man dogtrotted to the lodge and told what had happened to one of the managers, who called me in Red River, where I was employed as town marshal.

After hearing the pertinent information about the pesky bear, I suggested that the man and his wife bang pots and pans together to create enough noise to drive the bear away should it return. I really didn't think the bear would return after being hit by the rock, but I wanted to offer an alternate plan in case I was wrong. After giving what I considered good advice, I immediately forgot about the situation and went about my duties as town marshal.

Some time after midnight I was awakened by a call from one of the lodge's managers, who told me that he had one very scared tourist standing in his office nearly incoherent with fear. Needless to say, the bear had returned and the details went something like this.

Husband and wife, with pots and pans in hand, had walked onto the front porch and made a clatter. The bear had laid back its ears, woofed, and headed straight for the cabin door. They dropped the pots and pans, jumped into the cabin, and slammed the door shut. Just in time, too. The angry bear smashed the pots and pans and, deciding that was not enough, charged the front door, ripping off its screen and throwing it onto the yard with one well-aimed left hook. The bear threw its weight against the wood door, scratching off the door's paint and wood with its front claws. The door was so mangled it looked like someone had taken a chain saw to it. Fortunately, the front entrance to the cabin had been equipped with a drop crossbar for just such an emergency. The bear also knocked out the four small window panes in the top half of the door and then stuck its head through the opening to let out several tremendous roars, terrifying the family into frozen immobility. For some reason known only to the bear, it suddenly withdrew its head, walked calmly to the yard in front of the cabin, and sat down to ponder the situation.

Taking advantage of the break in action, the family moved furniture in front of the windows and door in case the bear returned. While they worked, the old sow sat on its backside in front of the cabin, occasionally raising its hind leg to scratch at a worrisome itch behind its right ear.

After about thirty minutes of inactivity, the bear casually walked to the east side of the cabin and started breaking out windows. Every time the bear smashed out a window it let out a thundering roar.

The man fought the bear with the best weapons he could find in the cabin—a rolling pin and a claw hammer. The bear did its best to climb through the frames of the smashed-out windows while the man did his best to beat the bear's head and front paws with the rolling pin and hammer, all of which had little effect except to possibly make the bear more angry.

Having worked up a thirst in its pursuit of the frightened family, the bear went to the river for a drink and to lie in its cool waters. Despite hitting the bear with some pretty hard licks with the hammer, the man was amazed to find no blood or hair on the hammer at all! He realized what little chance he and his family had if the bear got inside.

The man searched the house and found a five-inch two-by-four used as a cross-brace in one of the bed frames. He'd just pulled it loose when he heard glass breaking on the west side of the cabin and rushed in to find the furious bear trying once again to get through a window. The battle between man and beast raged for almost thirty minutes. The man later realized that what had actually saved the family from certain death was the very simple fact that the bear's girth exceeded the width of the window, making it impossible for it to get all the way through. "Thank God she was a fat one!" he told me.

About 6 P.M. the bear crossed Red River and lay under a tree. With a lull in the action, the mother very wisely consoled the two children, ages five and seven, and began to fix them supper—sandwiches of cold cuts and also potato salad left over from the noon meal. The bear strolled back to the cabin shortly before sundown and lay in front of the mangled cabin door. The family was trapped again.

The father had been exercising his brain to think of some possible way of getting to the lodge. As darkness fell, he searched every nook and cranny in the cabin. In one corner he found two bottle rockets and one M-80 firecracker left over from the Fourth of July celebration. While the children slept, he explained to his wife that they had only one chance, so they had to do it right. They both went to the front window and saw the bear lying peacefully on the porch. They decided surprise would be their best weapon. The father lit the fuse of one of the bottle rockets, and the rocket struck the bear in the rump and exploded with a sharp crack. The bear let out a bawl and headed for the river, then turned and stared at the cabin.

The man fired the second bottle rocket at the bear from a side window, but the rocket missed and exploded in the grass.

The bear sniffed at the exploded rocket and then headed to the cabin to lie on the front porch once again.

Deciding this was their last chance, husband and wife planned to distract the bear or scare it badly enough so that it would cross the river. The husband would then try to make a break for the lodge from the front door, and the wife would lock the door and lower its crossbar after the father left.

The husband, with folding buck knife in hand, stood ready to make his dash for the lodge some two hundred yards distant. His wife stood by the window, lit the M-80, and pitched it onto the bear's back. The bear jumped up and the firecracker rolled off onto the front step. As the bear sniffed at the sizzling fuse, the M-80 blew, burning the animal's whiskers and eyelashes. This definitely had an effect on the bear! It ran full speed to the river, jumped in, waded across, and disappeared into the darkness.

As soon as it crossed the river the father made his mad dash for the lodge. Upon arriving he discovered that the middle-aged couple who managed the lodge had locked up and gone to town for the evening. He looked for a window to gain entrance so he could use their phone, the only one in the area, but all the windows had safety screens installed in preparation for winter closing. The front door was not an option because it was locked with a regular night lock and deadbolt.

Knowing his family was relatively safe because of the bear's inability to get through the cabin windows, the father decided to wait for the return of the two managers. He put on an old coat he had found in an outbuilding, and he came upon a single-bit ax in the yard by the chopping block. He then climbed onto the roof of the lodge. Hoping against hope that the bear hadn't tracked him, he waited on the roof for three hours.

The couple came home at 11 P.M. to find the father sitting on the lodge roof with an ax on his lap! One of the managers, after warming up the shivering man, heard his story and called me. The manager explained that all he had in the way of armament was a .22 caliber rifle. I told him to forget about the rifle (which would be completely inadequate against a bear) and tell the father not to go back to the cabin.

I quickly got dressed, picked up my son's .30-30, and drove to the lodge in my patrol car. I picked up the tourist and together we drove to the cabin. The bear was nowhere in sight. I checked the .30-30 to make sure the magazine was full and that there was a round in the chamber. Using the patrol car's outside speaker, I told the mother to open the door.

I had never been so warmly greeted in my entire life! After the mother and children smothered the father with hugs and kisses, they turned their affection toward me. I had a child wrapped around each leg, and I was kissed by the mother three times before I could speak!

All talking at once, they told me what had happened, and I found it rather strange to hear four people so hoarse they could hardly speak. The mother said they had all screamed themselves silly from trying to scare the bear away and from their own sheer terror. I told them to get some sleep and that I would stand guard outside the cabin.

Though it was cold that night, I chose to sit in the open on a stump rather than in the cramped patrol car. The bear always came and went from the direction of the river, so I felt that if it came again it would be by the same route. I made myself comfortable and waited. At 2:30 A.M. I heard the gurgling of the river as a large animal waded across. Visibility was excellent because of the full moon, which illuminated the willow-lined riverbank for fifty or sixty yards. I raised the rifle to my shoulder.

The bear's form appeared on the edge of the river thirty yards from where I sat. I was going to use my five-cell flashlight, but as I looked down the barrel sights I realized I could clearly see the bear through the front sight by the light of the moon. I carefully squeezed the trigger.

The stillness of the mountain night was shattered instantly by the boom of my rifle and the roar of pain from the brownie, which took the .30 caliber 170-grain Silvertip squarely on the shoulder. Spinning away from the shot, the sow ripped up eight-foot willows that splashed into the river.

The river was relatively shallow in early fall and could be waded across at almost any point; the bear started to wade across near a narrow footbridge. Though I knew I was taking a chance, I sprinted directly for the footbridge, hoping to get a shot before the bear could either cross the river and possibly disappear into the woods or go down the center of the river to a bend forty yards distant. I had the rifle at my shoulder when I stepped onto the bridge.

For a split second the bear faced me from the middle of the river, then did a 180-degree turn and started splashing away downstream. I could tell the first shot had broken its left shoulder because its left leg was dangling helplessly. The angle of my shot was slightly above the bear. In the darkness I couldn't see my bottom sight clearly enough to take a shot at the back of its head, so I shot about three inches above the roof of the tail, hoping to break the bear's spine in the pelvic area. The shot had the desired effect, dropping the sow on its belly in the middle of the river. I knew I couldn't approach it from the river's banks because the willows along the banks would restrict my shooting ability. So I did the next best thing: I jumped off the bridge into two feet of icy river water and sloshed my way up alongside the bellowing bear.

Even though it couldn't move anything except its right front leg and its jaws, the bear's instinct to kill remained. It slapped the water with its right paw and its jaws snapped wildly. I fired into its right shoulder, the muzzle of the rifle a scant three feet away. The bear lay quietly in the water totally incapacitated yet still looking at me with a fierceness I will never forget. I mercifully ended its life with a bullet to the first vertebra joining the skull.

The bear was in perfect health and, except for having terrorized the family, was not known to be aggressive. What probably happened was that the bear became used to panhandling and took it badly when the family stopped feeding it.

I was generously thanked by the managers of the lodge and the family who had suffered through the terrible ordeal. But that was not all: My son benefited indirectly from the incident. Many of his friends had affluent parents who had bought their boys very expensive rifles, usually in .270, .30-06 or 7mm Remington Magnum calibers. He was the butt of quite a few jokes regarding his supposedly inadequate and obsolete .30-30 Winchester. I had purposely left my .338 on the rack, hoping I could dispatch the troublesome bruin with his rifle. My son was now the only kid in Red River who owned a rifle that had killed a dangerous bear!

That was one of only two bears that I ever had made into a rug, a tribute to a bruin that gave me some of the most exciting moments I'd ever had in a lifetime of hunting. The bear rug was placed on display for several years at the Sundance Wildlife Museum in Craig, Colorado.

Phantom Grizzly

People who aren't hunters have a somewhat misguided view of hunting. They tend to believe the only satisfying hunts must be those that end in a kill. Of course, if food is a necessity or if a bear is killing your sheep or cattle, the sooner the animal is killed the better. In sport hunting, however, the pressure is not that great and you can have a perfectly successful hunt without ever bagging a critter—especially when the animal proves a worthy antagonist, thwarting your purpose at every turn. The following is a story of a bear that bested me at my own game.

No words can describe the first three or four weeks of spring in the Cascade Mountains of central Washington. One can see magnificent snow-covered peaks and conifer-clad mountains that roll all the way to the horizon. It is the time of year when all creation seems glad to be alive. Everyday life is rejuvenated by the warmth of the spring sun. Certainly there could be no grander place to stand than on the southwestern slope of snow-peaked Mount Adams, which is where my story begins.

I had accepted an offer from two old lumberjack pals, Berl Thomas and Vernon Beeks, to visit them at their end-of-the-road camp on the west side of Mount Adams. Berl and Vernon were busily engaged in cutting a right-of-way for a new logging road into country where vehicular traffic had never been. The loggers had to "work wet" most of the day since the mountain slope was still covered with fast-melting snow, causing a thousand tiny rivulets to thread down the slope to the great rivers below.

Berl said that if I wanted to see a vista I would never forget, I should follow a certain trail to the edge of the timberline. Unable to resist, I started out just after breakfast, wearing snowshoes and carrying crampons in a light backpack to use when the going got icy.

After walking steadily for two hours, I came to a trail that was a regular animal turnpike. It was unusually wide for a timber trail and looked as though livestock had once traveled it. I knew this could not be the case, though, since it would be almost impossible to drive livestock through the heavy black timber to the mountain meadows above timberline. I turned left onto the trail, which gradually ascended to the northwest.

About noon I reached the timberline. Berl was right: The view was splendid, breathtaking! I sat down on a rock to eat lunch and to rest from the hard morning climb. In places the snow had melted off entirely, showing green shoots of alpine plants just beginning to emerge. I saw in the meadows long ribs of drifted snow up to three feet high. As I continued my hike, I came upon a drift that swept across the trail. The drift was too deep to break through, so I turned left and walked alongside it, looking for a place to cross. After walking around a large rock projection, I immediately noticed large bear tracks from what must have been a monster bear. I dropped to my knees to examine them.

The front pad was better than seven and a half inches across. If everything on the bear was in proportion to the paw, its hide would be eight to eight and a half feet long! Three and a half inches in front of the toe prints were indentations where claw points had pressed into the mud. I took a deep breath. This was no average bear but a huge grizzly—unbelievably large for a mountain grizzly! On Kodiak Island, located in the Gulf of Alaska and home to extremely large bear, this grizzly would not be considered a real trophy. Nonetheless, its tracks were unequivocally the largest I had ever seen from a mountain grizzly. I estimated that it weighed two hundred fifty to three hundred pounds *more* than the average mountain grizzly! The tracks were fresh, and I surmised that only the rock projection had hid it from my view. I checked my rifle to make sure I had a round chambered and started back down the drift, realizing that in a few minutes the grizzly would catch my scent and swiftly depart that area of the mountain.

You might think it would be easy to spot an eight-hundred-pound grizzly above timberline, but this is not always the case. There are numerous depressions in meadows and around streambeds as well as many convoluted rock formations that can serve as hiding places for a wise old grizzly.

I saw another rock projection twenty yards straight ahead and headed for it. The outcrop was four feet high and twelve feet long and jutted horizontally from the mountain slope. Feeling that my quarry was just on the other side of this formation, I circled thirty yards down the hillside to give myself enough room to get off a shot if it should charge. I rounded the corner of the rock expecting to see the grizzly at any moment. I saw nothing! Absolutely nothing! With my rifle at the ready, I walked straight up the 45-degree slope to the jutting rock. I found fresh scat, still steaming—left there, I presumed, by that contemptuous old griz!

I looked to the left and to the right of the rock, but I could find no tracks. I was beginning to become slightly unnerved by this strange turn of events, and I walked fifty yards down the hill to the corner of the outcrop. I stood for almost thirty minutes looking up where the grizzly had been only moments ago. I walked back up to the rock and noticed that the slope tapered far more gradually than I had thought. The ground was extremely hard there, too. I walked straight up the mountain almost seventy yards to where a drift crossed my path, and then I angled off to a stream some one hundred twenty yards downhill to my right. I looked at the rock formation where I had found the bear scat and still could not figure out how the grizzly had escaped—unless eight-hundred-pound grizzlies can become invisible and fly!

At least half a dozen times I hunted the southwestern slope of Mount Adams for that grand grizzly. I tracked it many times but never got as close as I had on that day. By the end of summer I knew the bear's color, weight, diet, habits, and trails, but I never laid eyes on it—not one time! I consider myself a far better than average bear hunter but this bruin sure skunked me—fair and square!

If I had seen the bear would I have shot it? Maybe—in the beginning—but after I got to know it, probably not. I grew mighty fond of the bear I couldn't see! Over the years I have thought about the animal many times and have always wished it well—wherever it might be.

Mosquito Pass, Colorado, 1956.

On the Yakima Indian Reservation, Toppenish, Washington, where I worked as a predator control hunter, 1964.

Marshal of Red River, with Floyd Biddie, my deputy, 1970.

The beginning of bear fever. My first bear, taken with help from Dad, 1953.

C. E. Barnett and I, with coyote, 1964.

Taking a shot at a coyote, 1969.

My son, Keith, and Eddie Gunyon, 1966.

Keith, all grown up, holding a .30-30, his boyhood rifle and the one I used to kill the bear described in "Red River Rampage," 1999.

My favorite rifle. A .270 Winchester cartridge in an FM Mauser, a sure killer in open country when loaded with 150-grain Noslers. The scope is a K-4 Weaver, also my favorite.

The bear responsible for the Red River rampage, one of only two I had made into a rug, 1999.

Father and son, 1996.

That's blood smeared on my forehead and cheek, a tradition among Indian hunters after killing bison or bear, 1989.

Jim Hasler and I with Jim's antelope, 1995. Jim was one of the hunters who helped me track the "Spirit Bear."

Parkinson's disease has made it impossible for me to hunt bear anymore, 1999.

The Bear with Personality

   I am one of the first to complain about those who attribute human characteristics and thoughts to wild animals. We often see this done in movies and television shows. I recently saw the movie *The Bear,* and in one scene a motherless cub befriends a giant bear that had been seriously wounded by a professional hide hunter. The little bear, making puppylike whimpers, snuggles up to the injured bear and licks tenderly at the ugly wound on its side.

   While that makes for a warm and fuzzy scene, it is also totally unrealistic. What really would have happened if the cub had approached the wounded and hungry bear? It would have been pinned to the ground by the massive paw of the injured bear, bitten through the shoulders, shaken like a rat, and eaten in short order. There is almost no reality in movies and televisions shows that feature animals.

   This is not to conclude, however, that animals don't now and then exhibit human traits. I don't pretend to be an animal behaviorist or biologist; still, I have observed animals all my life and am convinced that they can formulate a plan and then carry it out. They are also capable of showing affection for their family members and—on rare occasions—for a human being. This story is about a bear who, to use an Indian phrase, was "my brother under the skin."

C. E. Barnett and I were checking an area west of Toppenish, Washington, in the Signal Hill area of the Yakima Indian Reservation. We were looking for clues that would lead us to a stock-killing bear that had caused extensive depredation over a ten-mile radius. It was mid-June, and since coming out of hibernation the old sow had been raising Cain with stock for two and a half months. The sow had two, two-year-old cubs that it had run off when it was in season. We had seen neither the sow nor the two cubs, but the sow's tracks were found around every predatory kill. As much as we detested the practice of setting snares, C. E. and I deemed it necessary since the old sow was killing every day and never returning to a kill. The number of lost stock was increasing rapidly.

On June 17, C. E. and I were eating lunch on a ridge overlooking about a quarter-mile of creek bed approximately two hundred yards below. To our surprise we saw a limping bear making its way up the creek and headed for higher ground. We looked it over carefully with our binoculars and could see its muzzle covered with dried blood.

"C. E., we got lucky," I said. "What do you wanna bet that that's our killer?"

C. E. watched for a few seconds and replied, "I think that's her all right. I got the last one, you take this one."

From a sitting position I took steady aim with my Pre-'64 Feather Weight Winchester .270 and set off a 150-grainer. The Nosler Partition bullet smashed the bear's spine three inches in front of the shoulder. When we reached the sow we found it dead. It was indeed our stock killer. Its off-angled left front paw and broken claw on the right front toe matched exactly the tracks around the killed stock.

We carefully examined the carcass and learned that last fall it had been in a fight with a much larger bear that was trying to kill the sow's cubs. We now understood why it had been reduced to killing stock. The bear's body suffered several large lacerations and several tooth punctures that were badly infected. Its right front shoulder was dislocated, making any kind of movement unbelievably painful. The gangrenous flesh around the infected areas confirmed that its wounds had been with it throughout winter, probably making its hibernation a living nightmare. The crusted blood on its muzzle told us the bear had not had a chance to wash up after eating and that we would find a kill a short distance away. A quarter-mile downstream we found a partially eaten three-month-old calf that had been killed probably not more than a few hours before. Its body was still a little warm.

One of the two cubs, the little female, which the sow had run off, had been captured. It had been badly maimed by five or six of the shepherd's dogs, and the sheepherder had been forced to shoot it. The male cub, however, was still out there doing its best to survive.

We were in the process of picking up the bear snares we had set to catch the stock killer. We had only one more snare to pick up, set to the east of a small creek running over with brook trout. C. E. and I brought our fishing poles with the idea that we would have fresh trout for lunch. When we got to the snare we discovered, much to our surprise, that we had captured a dark brown bear of precisely the right age to be the missing cub of the stock-killing sow.

The cub was emaciated and had fought the snare for so long that he was barely able to make a sound or snap his jaws. We looked him over and discovered that both front paws were dripping yellow pus from infected wounds inflicted by numerous imbedded porcupine quills. His nose and upper and lower lips were also infected from imbedded quills. It was easy to understand why the cub was in such a sorry state. We surmised he had probably run into the porcupine shortly after his mother abandoned him in late May. After examining the cub, C. E. was of the opinion that he should be shot and put out of his misery. I confess that my tender-hearted side got the best of me and I suggested we operate on the little fellow.

C. E.'s first reaction was something like "Are you out of your mind!" But upon thinking it over further he agreed we should try to save the cub. I went back to the pickup truck to get our first-aid kit, which contained all the usual amenities as well as suture thread, three different types of needles, razor blades, and powdered sulfa packs, used during World War II and the Korean War. These items had been added to the kit so that if either C. E. or I were mauled in the field, we would have adequate means of doing on-the-spot emergency treatment.

We decided the best way to administer the first aid was to have C. E. hold the bear down with his gun while I performed the necessary surgery. I knelt beside the cub, still snared by his right hind paw, and talked to him gently and stroked his side. The little guy made no attempt to bite or scratch.

I used the razor blade to cut along the edges of the main pads and toe pads of the front paws to relieve some of the pressure, since the paws were distended from the pus inside. After opening the pads one at a time, I squeezed out the infection, washed the wound, applied sulfa powder, and sewed up the incision.

During the process, which took about two and a half hours, the only time the cub showed the slightest anger or fear was when I had to push the remaining quills all the way through his flesh to extract them. The cub responded only with a weak bawl and a sharp popping of the teeth. I then had to work on his muzzle and lips, which were thoroughly perforated and terribly swollen. This would be the tricky part, for I would be working close to those powerful jaws and sharp teeth.

After a twenty-minute break, I started splitting the lips and laying back the edges, similar to what a taxidermist does. I squeezed out the pus in one-inch increments, washed the wounds with peroxide, applied sulfa, and stitched the wounds closed. That took three hours, meaning I had spent a total of five and a half hours working on the young fellow. While I worked on the head, the cub never snapped or showed aggression. This seemed almost incredible since the pain must have been excruciating! Except for the occasional bawl, he had been very quiet—his eyes never leaving my face. Now I ask you: How would you responded to the same operation without anesthetic?

After finishing the first-aid treatment, I released the snare from around the cub's hind foot, hoping he would respond on his own, but he only lay there looking at me intently. C. E. made the suggestion that the cub was probably dehydrated from the ordeal and that he didn't have the strength to move. I sat down on the creek bank, put the cub's head in my lap, and very gently and very slowly trickled water from my canteen into his dry and swollen mouth. I did this for almost two hours, right up until sunset. We had both told our wives we might be out two days, so they would not be unduly concerned if we didn't return that evening. It wasn't hard to talk C. E. into spending the night.

While I had been pouring water down the little bear's mouth, C. E. had caught enough brook trout for supper for the three of us. We got our sleeping bags laid out in a comfortable position, and I carried the cub up to the campsite so I could keep an eye on him during the night. As weak and tired as he was, the little bear just couldn't resist the smell of fresh trout. Even though bears are not used to eating fried fish, I decided it would be tidier to hand-feed him with cooked fish rather than raw. I held his head in my lap and pinched off about one inch of fish flesh, placing the chunk in the bear's mouth. As painful as it must have been, he managed to eat two, eight-inch brookies. I checked on the cub several times during the night and gave him more water and fish. When I awoke I discovered the cub had crawled about a yard and a half to my sleeping bag and was lying snugly next to me.

Half the next day was spent watching the cub drink on his own, but the little guy was having a hard time getting to his feet. Several times I stood him up, and he would walk a few steps and collapse with a thump. C. E. and I decided the cub was mechanically sound but that the pain was too much for him to stay on his feet for more than a short period of time. We left him there on the creek bank with a cache of fish that should last him a week if he could defend the larder.

We returned the following week and sat around the camp until sunset, when our little pal put in an appearance. He looked much better and his wounds were healing nicely. (The thread used in the stitches was made of natural fibers that disintegrated over a period of time.) He sat politely on the opposite side of the campfire, and I occasionally pitched him a fish. C. E. and I were both aware of the inherent danger in feeding a wild bear from a campsite, but since this area of the reservation was totally uninhabited and seldom visited, we felt the risk to other humans negligible. As for C. E. and me, we would take our chances.

When I awoke in the morning, the two-year-old was lying by my side. He hung around camp during breakfast and left about one hour after sunup. This began one of the most interesting relationships a human being ever had with a member of the bear species.

During the remainder of summer when I patrolled the area, I would stop at our old base camp and within a few hours the bear, whom I had named Personality, would show up. I would fish and he would wait patiently nearby, observing my every move. He was always extremely well-behaved—never pushy and with a better disposition than most adolescents! He preferred his fish fried, and we always shared it equally.

When I sat by the campfire, he always watched me from the same spot—directly across from me with the campfire between us. He never infringed upon what he must have considered my personal space. I hated to see winter come because I thought I would never see him again. I said good-bye in late October after the first good snow had fallen, worried that he wouldn't survive the hard Cascade winter.

When spring came I couldn't wait to check on the cub. I now had a four-wheel-drive of my own, so I wouldn't have to rely on using the Indian reservation's vehicle or C. E.'s. Finally, the snow had cleared enough so that I could make it by road to the campsite by the first of June. During the long drive, I wondered if he was out of hibernation, but I also wondered if he was even still alive.

The camp itself had a southwest exposure and was relatively dry. I made a fire, then broke out my fishing pole and started catching brookies eager to nibble on anything that looked edible. In less than an hour and a half I had caught six, eight-inch brookies.

But there was no sign of Personality. I decided the best way to locate him was to cook the fish and allow the alluring scent to carry away into the forest. A young sow suddenly appeared with two tiny, just-out-of-the-den, roly-poly cubs. Well, I attracted a bear—just not the right one! I said "shoo" and it went *woof,* refusing to budge. It stood its ground about fifty yards from me and downwind of that tantalizing fish aroma. Suddenly from behind I heard a loud *woof,* which nearly scared the wits out of me! Strolling down to my right was Personality, much larger than the two-year-old I had met last fall.

During hibernation the bear had actually gained in size. With great dignity, he woofed again and the sow and cubs took off like a shot. If the sow had been older and more experienced, it might have taken exception to Personality's barging in on the scene. As it was, it decided discretion was the better part of valor and left for parts unknown. My bear watched the sow depart, and then he swaggered to the other side of the fire and dropped his rump with a thump in the usual spot. He raised one paw to signal it was time for a fish—or maybe he was just saying hi.

Over the years he grew into a four-hundred-pound blackie. Without fail he always meet me near our spot and was always a large-hearted gentleman in my presence. He came into camp even when C. E. was there but would not come if C. E. was alone at camp. Perhaps he remembered that C. E. had held a gun on him the day I performed the ad-lib operation that, no doubt, saved his life. The occasional sheepherder moving his flock through the area could have posed a threat, but Personality never showed himself and never resorted to eating sheep.

My job assignment in Washington State finally ended, and I told C. E. and Eddie Gunyon, one of my Indian police friends, that I wanted to make one last trip alone to the old campsite for sentimental reasons. They both understood as only men wise to woodland ways could.

That day with my bear was like a fairy tale, one of those rare occasions when there's pure magic in the air. We walked up and down the trail together as we had many times in the past. While I sat at camp relaxing, Personality stood and gazed intently at my face, the dying embers of the campfire between us. He knew what I couldn't tell him: This was the last time we would be together. "Good-bye," I said quietly, and with a very soft *woof* he turned and walked out of my life forever. My physical life, that is.

A couple years later, C. E.'s job assignment also ended in Washington, and just before he left he wrote to say that he had recently seen Personality. He said the bear looked healthy and now weighed a full five hundred pounds. A real mountain king!

I know people laugh at the old television show *Grizzly Adams*, which depicted a close, personal relationship between a man and a bear. As I stated at the beginning of this chapter, I too have many reservations about the way bears have been depicted in movies and television series. But, at the same time, I believe a bear is capable of at least some emotions we might rightly call human. This may sound crazy, but I believe Personality was in some inexplicable way my brother—covered in bearskin.

Lesson Learned

While my family and I lived in Cortez, Colorado, I became friends with Dick Sanders, a government trapper living near Mancos, and we hunted together whenever circumstances would allow. In early October 1965, we were trying to trap or kill a wily old coyote named Three Legs that had been terrorizing domestic sheep near Mancos River Canyon. Dick and I were enjoying the warm Indian summer, soaking up sunrays as we ate lunch and talked about our strategy for the afternoon hunt.

Earlier that day, Dick had mentioned that there was another predator out there: a female black bear that had been killing sheep for about three weeks at the rate of one a day. He suggested I keep an eye out for the bear, easily identifiable because of its almost blond fur. I began to wish I had brought a different loading for my new rifle, a Pre-'64 Winchester Model 70 in .264 Magnum caliber. The only shells I had were 100-grain Winchester Power-Points, great for blowing up coyotes but not what one would use for tackling a two-hundred-fifty-pound bear. Dick and I decided that the high-velocity 100-grain bullet would probably have enough punch to bring down a bear hit in the lungs or heart.

As we were about to begin our hunt, Dick said with a mischievous smile, "I'll trade you rifles." I made some smart remark about his .250-3000 Savage not being any better than my .264, nor was it nearly as pretty. "Now, don't get smart!" replied Dick with a laugh. "This old .250-3000 has killed a lot of game!" He was right about that. I truly believe that that rifle has killed more deer, antelope, and coyote than any other .250-3000 in existence.

Dick and I split up to check the coyote traps, which were spread throughout the canyon. Over a period of several hours I checked eight sets, finding a coyote in three of them but no Three Legs.

About 3:30 P.M. I heard a lamb's cry and was sure within a matter of seconds I would see Three Legs in the vicinity. I ran thirty yards to the hill's crest and searched the sage on the valley floor. I could see panicked sheep running in every direction. Having been preoccupied with looking for Three Legs, I at first overlooked the real culprit. The blond bear that Dick told me about was making off with a half-grown lamb, which was hanging limply from the sow's mouth. The bear was headed toward the pinon- and juniper-covered hillside. I dropped to a sitting position and lined up the bear in my peepsight. The shot looked good and there was nothing left to do but squeeze, but at that moment I heard a voice whisper, "Don't, don't, don't." I looked up from the sights and watched the bear disappear into the junipers. The whisper in my ear at that last second had made me question the efficacy of hammering a bear from the backside with that tiny 100-grain varmint bullet. Experience told me not to take that shot.

I sat there on the hillside not moving for almost forty-five minutes, wondering what the best approach might be to the densely treed side canyon that the bear had scampered into. As the shadows lengthened, the air began to cool and the two-to-three mile-per-hour breeze changed direction. It was now blowing squarely in my face as I started up the side of the juniper-choked opening to the side canyon. I felt relieved knowing the bear could not possibly pick up my scent, for I was perfectly downwind from my quarry.

After proceeding four hundred yards into the canyon, I was nearing the top of the draw when I distinctly heard the breaking of bone directly ahead. I knew I was within one hundred yards of the feeding bear. Few trees grew near the top of the canyon, which meant I would have a relatively clear shot. I took a tangent slightly to my left that angled upward to the highest point of elevation on my side of the canyon wall. I had been walking on loose and rolling rocks almost all the way up but had not dislodged a single one. But then a softball-sized rock shot out from under me and bounded down the side of the steep canyon wall. I was cursing myself as well as Murphy for always being on the job. Wouldn't you know it—just when silence was most important!

I froze in my position and waited to see what the bear would do with the information the rolling rock had given it. I stood like a statue for ten minutes, watching the mouth of the canyon. The only sound was the squawking of a distant magpie. Whatever the bear was doing, it was being very quiet about it.

Then, to my left one hundred yards away, I saw an ear, an eye, and, finally, the nose of the blond bear peeking from behind an eight-foot-square rock on the hillside. It couldn't see me, I was sure of that, and it definitely couldn't smell me, but it was sure something was out there. The waiting game went on for at least another ten minutes, and I was becoming very cramped and uncomfortable—frozen in the open under the sow's searching scrutiny. "Move, you old sow," I mumbled. "I can't stand like this much longer."

The bear took a step forward and looked up to where the canyon was at its highest. Immediately I dropped to a kneeling position, slipped off the safety, and began my trigger squeeze–the sights lined up on the bear's spine just in front of the shoulder. But then the bear turned its head to my left, taking away the only shot I felt sure would kill instantly with that tiny bullet. I held my kneeling position for at least another five minutes–neither of us moving–when suddenly the bear's head swung back, looking almost directly at me but with its nose slightly to my right.

The waiting game had taken its toll on my nerves. I knew the shot had to be made now or never, for my hands and arms were beginning to tremble when I aimed the rifle. It would have been a relatively easy shot if I had been using a four-power scope, but with the rifle's steel peepsights the shot was going to be a little harder.

I reasoned that the only way I could be sure of a quick kill was to slip the 100-grain missile into its left eye socket. The bullet would then travel into the bear's brain, killing it instantly. The crack and recoil of the firing rifle disturbed my sight picture, but I still felt the shot went precisely where I had aimed. The blond sow dropped as if struck by lightning, and I stood up and started to walk to where it lay. But as quickly as it had gone down, it was back up and bawling in rage and wiping the blood off its face with its left paw. Then Murphy did it again. My left foot rolled on a rock and I fell flat on my back with a thud on the steep hillside. For a moment I could hardly catch my breath and–wouldn't you know it–the angry bear had located my position and was headed my way! I have never seen a bear bawl so loudly during a charge. From a seated position, I aimed again at the left eye socket and squeezed off the shot. The bear went down on its nose, but it was up again before I could cycle the bolt.

The blond bear was at the bottom of the canyon and starting up the incline on my side. It suddenly dawned on me that it was only fifty yards away and I had only two shells left. I again placed the rifle's front bead on the left eye socket and fired. Upon receiving this bullet the bear bawled pitifully and spun 360 degrees. I was still sitting and the bear was twenty yards away and still charging! Strings of saliva were flying from both sides of its mouth. A bloody spray was flying back over its shoulder from its terrible scalp wound. Its muzzle was turned to the far left so that its right eye could fasten directly on me.

The remainder of the encounter unfolded as if in slow motion. I felt no panic. I was strangely detached—as if it were all happening to someone else. Even though I knew I needed to hurry, I felt no rush. For the fourth time I lined up on its left eye, the beast fifteen yards distant. I heard a voice in my head say *Now*. I felt the rifle's recoil. I did not hear the report of the rifle, nor did I hear the animal's bawl. The bear's nose plowed into the loose shale.

There lay the bloody sow, a scant ten yards away! I don't know how long I sat there contemplating what might have been. I started to get up but didn't have the strength. My legs were rattling so badly I couldn't walk for fifteen minutes.

When I finally examined the bear, I discovered it was about nine years old and in very good health, with the exception of having six or seven large porcupine quills broken off in its upper lip and nose. This, no doubt, caused it great pain and probably led it to kill sheep, which are easy prey. I also noticed that the last 100-grain bullet had hit the arch above the left eye and the first three had hit in exactly the same spot. The fact remains, though, that the first three shots exploded on the bone without entering the skull cavity—that is why you don't want to be shooting big game with lightweight bullets! The shards of flying copper and lead had totally demolished the eyeball to give the bear a ghastly appearance but did nothing more than make it terribly angry. The last shot, deliberately taken, entered the eyeball socket and proceeded to the back of the skull. A later postmortem revealed that the brain had been totally destroyed and so had the 100-grain bullet.

I was surprised to discover the base of a bullet sticking out approximately an eighth of an inch from the right side of the bridge of the bear's nose. I learned after removing the bullet with my pocketknife that it was an 87-grain .25 caliber almost totally intact.

On the way home that evening I showed Dick the .25 caliber bullet. He got a surprised look on his face, slapped his leg, and laughed long and loud. "You know something, partner?" he said. "I shot a bear two years ago about twenty miles from here and it got away after I thought I'd made a perfect head shot. I never saw the bear again and just figured it had gone off somewhere and died. This has to be the same bear!"

"You know, Dick," I said, "looks like a couple of old hunters like us would know by now to use enough gun and—more important—enough bullet to get the job done."

"I'll say amen to that!" said Dick.

I guess you live and learn, because the next time we hunted together I was carrying my .270 with 150-grain Noslers and Dick was carrying his new .308 Savage loaded with 180-grain Noslers. The blond-bear fiasco was the last time either of us ever attempted to shoot a bear without using enough caliber and bullet.

Spirit Bear

In fall 1962 I found myself sitting on a bed of pine needles watching an old Yakima Indian perform an ancient ritual. Earlier that day, the Indian had killed a bear with a single shot from a seven-and-a-half-inch-barrel .45 Colt Peacemaker. The old Indian smoked his sacred pipe and prayed, hoping his prayer would find favor with the great Spirit Bear, the Father of all bears. He thanked the animal for its claws, tallow, hide, and all the rest that would be made use of during the coming winter; then he blew smoke into the bear's nostrils to sanctify its internal organs. By thanking the bear for these great and precious gifts, the bear's spirit would know that its body parts would not be wasted. They would all be used thankfully.

Two hours into the ritual, the medicine man turned to me and said: "You are the bear hunter that has been appointed to slay the troublesome bears in the mountains that the bear and I call home."

I was surprised by this statement, for he had never seen me before and could not have known my occupation or why I had come.

"The eagle carried a vision to me of you coming up the trail below the falls," he continued, "so I knew you were the man that Eddie Gunyon had spoken of. You are the hunter the tribal elders had hired so that the Basque herders could renew their lease to herd sheep on Indian land. I knew why you were here because you were part of a vision given to me many years ago." After a pause the Indian said, "Tell me, why have you come to see me?

"Eddie thought it best that I come to you to receive a blessing," I said, "so that no harm would come to me while doing the job of thinning out the bears."

He looked at me intently and said: "I read in your eyes that you do not hate bears; you love them more than any other animal. With such a feeling in your heart, I will make magic that will protect you all of your days. As long as you remember your heritage, no bear will harm you. With the help of this bear," continued the Indian, pointing at the bear carcass, "we will make the protecting medicine: we three—the bear, the seer, the hunter."

I was moved beyond words and sat with the medicine man for another hour. When the ceremony was over, the Indian said: "Young man, for twenty years I have waited for this day," then added cryptically: "I won't be alive to see the end of your story, but I know the outcome. When you have completed your work here, come see me and I will tell you the rest of my vision."

It took three years to thin out the bears, and before I left Yakima Valley, which is located in the Cascades Mountains in Washington, I went to see the old Indian. He told me that he had known from the very beginning that I was a quarter-breed Comanche and that my Spirit Guide was the eagle and that my Totem was the grizzly bear. He also told me about my final hunt, which, as it would turn out, included an eagle and a grizzly.

My tale begins in 1986 while hunting with my friend Chuck Taylor during spring bear season . As I mentioned earlier, when I hunt in Craig, Colorado, I often use the McAnally home as a base. The McAnallys live near a valley on the northwest end of Black Mountain, northeast of Craig. The valley extends from Fortification Creek to Sand Point. The area resembles a large bowl, bound on the north by Mount Welba, on the south by Mount Oliphant, and on the west by Sand Point. Most of the bowl contains blue spruce, some aspen, and many small meadows. The basin is also home to many bear. Even though the thaw was well under way, the weather for spring bear season that year was horrendous. It rained every day, making hunting in the bowl miserable at best.

Since Chuck and I were bait hunting, I had been using several kinds of scents, including oil of anise, honey, Limburger cheese, and stale pastries from our local bakeries. We had several bears come to the baits, but none had come during daylight hours, which was the only time we could legally hunt bear. Moreover, we could not track our daytime visitors because the rains obliterated the tracks.

Chuck could not stay for the whole of bear season, so Jim Hasler became my new hunting partner. Chuck and I had baited one particularly good area with bacon grease in a lard can, and on consecutive nights a bear had emptied the can. Jim and I continued to use the same procedure, but time was running out. The bear had not been seen during shooting hours, and on the last day of bear season the critter left us a real teaser. We found that the lard can had been cleaned out, as usual, but this time the animal was apparently angry that there was no more and in frustration bit across the can's circumference. It left a set of teeth marks and three claw scratches on the bottom where it had tried to wipe out the last residue with its paw. The tantalizing thing about the claw marks was that there were only three: The bear's paw was wider than the width of the open lard can. The mouth of the can was six inches across!

I took the can home to measure the distance between the tooth punctures of the upper and lower jaws. Next, I went to the taxidermy shop and started measuring bear skulls and bite distances. I discovered that the jaws of the bear were a third wider than that of any skull in the shop, the largest there belonging to a five-hundred-pound bear killed two years earlier. As a point of reference, I measured the bite width of my sixty-pound collie, finding that the bite width of the bear was two and a half times wider. This was one whale of a big bear!

When bear season rolled around again in spring 1987, that area of Black Mountain was hunted extensively by Jim Hasler, Bob Aaberg, and me. All we got for our trouble, though, was the finding of a bear track in the sand. Basing our estimates on the size of the track, we believed we were hunting a bear that would square at about seven feet, four inches and weigh in the neighborhood of six hundred pounds.

We hunted the giant bear for five more seasons before another clue turned up—a perfectly clear front track from which I could take a perfect measurement. The bear had grown, its front track now an even seven and a half inches. This meant it would most likely square eight and a half feet and weigh as much as eight hundred pounds. We deduced that it was probably in perfect condition, for we could detect no abnormality in its stride. We still didn't know its color because of the remarkable absence of its hair on trailside trees, which bears tend to rub against as they pass.

I knew that Bob and Jim were excited by the prospect of getting a shot at such a huge bear, but to me it became an obsession. During those years the bear came to our baits many times, but not once did any of us lay eyes on it. At least two other hunters, Stan McAnally and Hank Vallejos, saw the bear, though not during hunting season or when they were armed.

Stan McAnally said that a hummingbird feeder on the front porch of his home had been a frequent dessert stopover for the big bear. It didn't have to tear up the feeder to drink from it, either. The bear simply stood flat on its hind feet and very gently tipped the feeder with its forepaws and lapped the contents until the feeder was dry. The feeder was about seven feet above ground!

Hank Vallejos, who lived in the cabin below the McAnally's, had walked out one morning and started to climb into his three-quarter-ton GMC pickup, which also had a fold-down camper on the back. He was startled out of his wits to see a bear looking at him over the top of the camper! When I asked Hank what he did next, he said: "I just turned right around and went back into the house and waited two or three hours before attempting to go to town again."

No less than forty-seven times my baits had been raided by that bruin, but not once during daylight hours. Finally, in desperation, I attached an old alarm clock to the monofilament line I used when bait hunting. When the line would jiggle as the bear fed, I rigged it so that the movement would cause the clock to shut off. After repeating the experiment several times, I learned that, without fail, the bear had fed between 1 and 3:30 A.M. There was also another fact that I had learned about its eating habits: Until 1991, there was no evidence that it had ever killed domestic sheep.

Over the next three years, three other hunters—Kevin Brown, Wanda Brown, and Lynn Belleville—joined me in the hunt. Word had gotten out about the huge bear on Black Mountain, and a number of other good hunters also started looking for it. But none came close to the success I had managed to achieve.

In 1994, spring bear season in Colorado was abolished, leaving only one month of bear hunting in the fall, which was never as productive as bear hunting in spring. Moreover, I knew my hunting days were numbered. I had been diagnosed with Parkinson's disease in 1987, and by 1994 the physical demands of hunting were almost too much. So when fall bear season rolled around, I was desperate to bag this huge black bear. Its hide, after all, could set a world record and therefore be the crowning achievement of my bear hunting career.

Over the years the big bear made more and more forays out of its old haunts and into the area surrounding Four Mile Creek. This led me to expand my hunting area to the densely timbered basin over the rim of the bowl west of Sand Point and into the Four Mile Creek water course, which runs almost due west off Black Mountain to the prairie. The bear still had not angered the sheepherders and cattlemen because it usually left domestic stock alone. We found, though, many kills of deer and elk, which, to say the least, are highly unusual prey for a black bear.

I now knew the bear as well as anyone could without seeing it. I knew where it ate, day and night. I knew its habits almost as well as I know my own. I knew its hair was chocolate brown. All that was left was to see it long enough for me to pull the trigger.

Toward the end of the 1994 fall season, I was about worn out. I had to limit my walking when I hunted to no more than two miles a day, and I resorted to doing a lot of bear calls in an attempt to lure the bruin to me. My knowledge of the bear's eating habits was not helping because the berry and acorn plants on which it normally fed were not plentiful due to a late spring freeze. I had just about given up when one day, at 9:45 A.M., there was a breakthrough.

I was hunting with Kevin Brown, a local guide, and his wife, Wanda, both of whom are real outdoor people. It was a beautiful fall day, unseasonably warm for mid-September. There is no lovelier place in the world than Colorado in the fall. Huge patches of aspen gold were intermingled that day with the grayish green and greenish black of spruce, and the oak brush added a touch of reddish brown to the scenery. We were traveling a trail on Four Mile Creek and had gone about three-eighths of a mile. It was very late in the morning to try my call, but I decided to try it anyway.

I had stationed Kevin at the northwest corner of a meadow near the headwaters of a streambed. Wanda and I went forty yards farther in a southeasterly direction to where the trail entered a meadow. Wanda sat down in a depression three yards to my left rear so that I would not have to be concerned about her position. I could swing my rifle 360 degrees without putting her in the line of fire. I had only blown the call three times when down a narrow aisle through the aspens I suddenly saw my prize. Thirty-five yards away between two trees was the black bear looking me squarely in the eye.

I raised the .358 Winchester, loaded with 225-grain bullets. The cross hairs settled on the ball joint of the bear's shoulders. The bear took two steps forward, so I moved the cross hairs six inches to a point just behind its shoulders—still plenty good for a shot. I felt for the first time the bear was mine.

I had a half-pound pull left on the trigger when the bear suddenly moved forward three feet, showing me nothing but its rib cage and part of its huge potbelly. Less than half a second more and I would have sent a bullet crashing into it. All I saw after that was the rear end of a northbound bear.

I'd been standing with my rifle pointed in the direction of the bear for eight to ten seconds, but it seemed more like an eternity. I whispered to Wanda, "Did you see him?"

"See what?" she asked.

"Didn't you see him? It was the big bear!"

"No. I saw you point the rifle but I didn't see a thing. I wondered what you were pointing at."

Then I realized those few yards separating Wanda and me made it impossible for her to see the great bear.

Instead of leaving that location or calling Kevin to tell him about the bear sighting, I stayed in the area for another thirty minutes to hunt the bear—though I knew it was useless because the bear was well aware of the presence of Wanda and me. Finally I notified Kevin of the sighting and that I thought it would be a good idea if we stayed on the trail and followed it around the curve into the black timber. This would put the bear downwind.

The plan was that I would lead, with Wanda about five steps behind me and Kevin ten behind Wanda, thereby covering both ends of the trail. Thus, if the bear attacked, we could fire at it from different angles. As we slowly walked about another half-mile, I heard sounds that only a seasoned bear hunter would hear. Occasionally the breeze swirled, bringing the bear's scent to me. I caught its scent no less than five times and am convinced it was never more than fifty yards from our hunting party at any time. We arrived at a place where heavy black timber grew close to the trail's edge, and knowing that the bear had been following us, I felt it would be imprudent to go farther. With Kevin and Wanda along I didn't want to chance it.

I told Kevin that I thought we might have one small chance to get the bear. The plan was for him to go back to the meadow where I had first seen the bear and find a position at the upper end that allowed him to see clearly the area where the trail opened into the meadow. Wanda and I would start out thirty minutes after Kevin. My hope was that the bear would stay with Wanda and me by paralleling us on the trail. As we neared the meadow, it might come out into the open long enough for Kevin to take a shot. While walking toward the meadow, Wanda and I caught the bear's scent several times, but the bear never showed itself.

Several days later I went hunting with Lynn Belleville, a true mountain man in every sense, in the Four Mile Creek country. We parked the vehicle at a saddle on the same ridge where I'd seen the bear a few days earlier. To the left of the saddle was the trail Wanda and I had followed when I had seen the bear. To the right was open ground that curved to a point, then dropped off abruptly to Fortification Creek.

From that point, you have unlimited visibility for four hundred yards to the south, eight hundred fifty to the west, and five hundred to the northwest. Lynn said he would descend the canyon from the point and come up the canyon's black-timbered side directly across from and to the south of where I would be. I hoped the bear would move out of the black timber, where it usually bedded down during the midday heat. I might possibly get a shot just before sundown.

The rest of the afternoon passed with nothing occurring of special interest, and as the sun began to set I headed back to the saddle. Less than two hundred yards from the vehicle, the trail passed between a grove of stunted aspen on the right and a sixty-yard band of almost impenetrable oak brush on the left. I caught the scent of the bear in the wind coming out of the southwest. I was downwind of it and hoped it would finally make a mistake and cross the forty yards of open trail in front of me. I waited without moving a muscle, but then the breeze began to swirl. Instead of blowing from the southwest, it eddied back and forth across the upper end of the valley. Almost directly in front of me I heard a *woof.* The eddying breeze had carried my scent to the quarry.

Now each of us knew exactly where the other was. As incredible as it may sound, over the next thirty minutes we were never more than twenty yards apart and sometimes much closer—me on the trail, the bear in the brush. For those thirty minutes I held my rifle to my shoulder and sidestepped the length of the oak grove, believing any moment the bear would make its move. Step for step the animal paralleled me the length of the oak patch, but not once did I see it. There was only the constant smell, the frequent *woof,* and the occasional popping of its jaws to let me know it was still with me. With only fifteen minutes of shooting light left, my nerves could take it no longer. I reluctantly left the brush and walked the remaining one hundred yards of open ground to the pickup truck. Lynn showed up several minutes later and I told him of the events over the last hour.

"Damn! That must have been exciting!" he said.

Exciting was not quite the right description. It was probably the most intense thirty minutes of hunting man or beast I have ever experienced. I called off the hunt for the next day; my shoulders were so painful I couldn't raise the Ruger 77 to sighting level because of those torturous thirty minutes when I held it to my shoulder, ready to fire at any moment.

During the one-day hunting break, an eerie feeling somewhat akin to déjà vu came over me. I remembered the old Indian's vision, seeing him in my mind's eye sitting cross-legged and telling me how my hunting days would end. I tried to put it out of my mind but could not. Next morning I said to Lynn, who was knowledgeable about Indian religion and philosophy: "Let's watch for any Indian omens that might appear during the trip and not ignore their portent." Lynn looked vaguely disturbed but agreed that no sign should be overlooked.

We were driving up Wilderness Ranch Road to our usual parking spot on Four Mile Creek when suddenly a golden eagle dived at the pickup truck, circled slowly three times, called three times, and flew to a spot over some aspens about sixty yards distant. It then repeated the scene there and flew into the valley.

Lynn looked at me and I looked at him and he said, "Better take a look, huh boss?" He jumped out of the truck and headed for the spot in the aspen grove. He returned shortly thereafter and said, "I don't understand this. There's a fresh mountain lion kill of a medium-sized doe. What's that got to do with the bear?"

"The eagle's trying to slow us down, Lynn! Hurry! Let's get up there!"

Approximately 1:30 P.M. we parked the truck in the usual spot in the middle of the saddle. As soon as we got out of the truck the overwhelming smell of the bear hit our nostrils. Since there was about a ten-mile-per-hour breeze from the southwest, we realized we were directly downwind of the bear and that it had just gone over the high point to our right some sixty yards distant. The scent was so pungent we knew the bear was only seconds ahead.

We took off at a run toward the point. Lynn, much younger than I and not crippled by Parkinson's disease, was nearing the summit well ahead of me. I yelled, "Watch it, Lynn! Careful when you go over the top!" The summit was only ten yards wide. If the bear was crossing the point when Lynn arrived, Lynn would be in immediate jeopardy. I could see Lynn stop at the point, look all around, and then look to the ground. When I arrived Lynn pointed to the ground and said, "Look right here!" A yellow pool of liquid was evaporating in a depression in the sand. Once we took a whiff, we knew what it was.

I was totally winded and sat down on a rock to catch my breath and to try to figure out where the bear could possibly have gone. Picture the knob where we were: scant brush, stunted cheat grass one and a half to two feet high, windblown sage.

There was no place a bear could hide within four hundred yards. For five minutes neither of us said anything, until I saw something incredible—a waterfowl three feet away under the sagebrush. I asked Lynn if he saw what I saw. Lynn's mouth dropped open. "That's a coot! That's a damn coot!" he said.

"What do you think?" I asked.

"What in the hell is he doing up here?"

After a long pause, I said: "Maybe his wing was injured in flight and he had no choice but to land here."

"I don't know about that," Lynn stammered, "but I'm leaving you with your little friend and gettin' the heck off this mountain. I'll go down into the valley, just like we did the other day, and work my way back to the pickup. See you 'bout dark." Lynn descended the hillside at a trot.

The short hairs on my neck stood up and a slight chill passed over me. Not knowing what else to do, I began talking to the coot: "What's the matter, little fella? You hurt your wing and can't fly or something?"

The coot took a couple steps out from under the sagebrush, cocked its head, and fixed its red eye on me. Then it went through a complete set of wing stretches, as if to show it was in perfect flying condition. After we eyed each other for three or four minutes, I said to the bird, "I've gotten your message." Apparently satisfied, the bird jumped into the head wind and flew away. Now, every outdoorsman knows that coots don't jump but run to become airborne. Eagles jump!

Alone now, I began to reflect on my forty-one years of bear hunting, and I remembered the old Indian. "Is this how it ends?" I whispered.

It did not take long, however, for me to slip back into the mind of the hunter. First unconsciously, I began to scan every inch of the sixty yards of cheat-grass hillside from the saddle to the summit. I was determined to find tracks, or get a serious case of eyestrain trying. I got down on my hands and knees, for as any good tracker knows, when you lower your head to ground level you pick up things you otherwise miss while looking from an upright position. Suddenly I saw three toe prints in the hard ground. Then I saw the print of the left front paw. Gazing

HUME 99

intently just ahead and to the right about two and a half feet, I saw the imprint of the right front paw, its entire width and shape clearly visible to the trained observer.

I took out my folding knife. Knowing the knife was exactly six inches, I used it to measure the tracks; then I lay on my back and laughed. This was my bear, all right. It had gotten even bigger over the last four years since I had last seen a complete, measurable track. These tracks measured around eight and a quarter to eight and three-eighth inches across. I built a little fence of rocks around the tracks to mark them in case Lynn should return before nightfall.

I tried to visualize the path the bear had taken when it left the point. Suddenly I noticed something. In the worn-down, windblown cheat grass there were two lines paralleling each other about four or five feet apart, creating an erratic zigzag. I looked closer and, now knowing what to look for, saw the zigzag as clear as day. Lynn returned close to sundown, and when I pointed out the zigzag he didn't know what to make of it.

"Come on, Lynn," I said, "you know what those lines are. I know you've seen mountain lion and bear kills after the predator had moved the kill to a safer place."

His eyes began to shine. "I know what they are. They're drag marks."

"Right on! You win the prize!"

Mountain lion will usually drag its kill on the outside of its shoulder or between its front legs by holding the carcass in its jaws and towing it to the desired location. Bear, by contrast, especially large ones, will clamp its jaws on the prey's spine behind the shoulders, lift the entire animal off the ground, and carry it so that only its paws or hooves touch the ground.

The tracks from the bear's front pads measured over eight inches across, and the distance between the tracks was about two and a half feet. From this we could easily deduce that this bear now weighed over a thousand pounds, capable of carrying a full-grown deer or yearling elk with nothing but the hooves touching the ground. Awesome!

I couldn't make it to the point during the last two days of bear season. I was exhausted physically and emotionally. On the last day of the season I received a call from Kevin Brown. He said that he and Wanda planned to walk the trail all the way around the loop, cross the canyon, and proceed to the point, an all-day hike. I told him I'd like to go but didn't have the strength. I also told him that they should stay out of the black timber on the other side of the canyon because the tightly packed timber allowed for no shooting room at all.

On the evening of the last day of bear season, I received another phone call from Kevin. Having a mind of their own, he and Wanda had walked the trail precisely through the darkest part of the black timber, just what I told them *not* to do. He was so excited he could hardly contain himself! He said he had found an aspen tree where a huge bear had stood on its hind legs and stretched to its full length. Its claw marks were made as high as it could reach up the tree. The only way he could measure the height was to hold the rifle in his right hand with his finger in the trigger guard and reach up, with the barrel of the rifle extending to the claw marks. Using as a measuring stick his height—five feet, ten inches—Kevin determined that the bottom of the claw mark was ten and a half feet from the ground. He went on to say that the front paws were spread out, since the bear had dug its claws into the tree and stretched and pulled. The front track was naturally spread out, the distance between the claw marks being a full two inches. This meant that the extended paw was around eleven inches wide. When you have time, measure ten and a half feet on the side of your house. You'll readily agree that it would take one very large bear to make scratches that high.

What do I know for sure about the giant bear?

(1) Its fur is chocolate brown.
(2) Its track is eight and a quarter to eight and three-eighth inches wide.
(3) Its width between the tread is two feet, six inches.
(4) Its stretch is ten and a half feet.
(5) It can carry a calf-elk carcass with only the hooves dragging.

This evidence indicates several indisputable facts. Its hide would square over nine feet, not only making it a huge mountain grizzly but also placing it in the category of a trophy-sized Alaska brown bear. When the bear comes out of its den it'll weigh nine hundred to nine hundred sixty pounds, and when it returns there in early winter it'll weigh, assuming the summer was good, twelve to thirteen hundred pounds.

* * * * * *

I clearly remember what the old Yakima Indian said to me in 1965, after I had thinned out the bears on the reservation. "You are a great bear hunter, blessed with the gift of knowing his mind and his ways. But the day will come when you will no longer hunt bears."

"How will I know that I have hunted my last bear?" I asked.

"The great Spirit Bear—the Father of all bears—will make himself known to you. He will tell you that the end of your hunting days has come."

That day in fall 1994 turned out to be my last bear hunt. I didn't draw a bear tag for the 1995 season. Parkinson's disease had weakened me to the point that hunting in mountainous terrain was out of the question. By 1999, hunting had become impossible. I still hope to make it back to Black Mountain to meet the great bear one last time, but not as a hunter. I would meet him as a friend, my soul at peace with his.

Bear Rifles and Cartridges

I realize I am opening a can of worms when I start talking about what is an adequate bear rifle and what is not. If this is the case, so be it! Let the worms wiggle! Every hunter has an opinion—sometimes justified, sometimes not—but facts are hard to ignore.

A number of years ago a noted deer hunter wrote a nice article on the .243. He stated that the .243 loaded with 90-grain bullets or heavier was adequate for any mule deer that walked the continent under 90 percent of the conditions encountered in the field. I'm not here to argue the validity of that claim, but when I had the opportunity to question him a month or so after the article appeared, his answer astounded me.

"How many deer did you shoot with the .243 to make such a grandiose claim for that caliber?" I asked.

He looked me right in the eye and said, "Three."

I about passed out! Three one-shot kills is hardly enough evidence from which to formulate a conclusion. Since then I've learned to take what I read with a grain of salt.

In this chapter I will offer plenty of evidence for why I prefer certain rifles and cartridges over others. I will also discuss the best rifles, cartridges, and bullets to be used on bear. I will be rather dogmatic about my opinions and, as my friends know, I am not easily swayed. If you plan to hunt bruin—large or small—the information I give you may someday save your life.

When choosing a rifle, I make sure it has one of three types of actions. I like the single drop block, such as the Ruger No. 1, Winchester High Wall, and the Sharps original buffalo shooters. I also like a good lever action, specifically Winchester models 71, 86, 94, and the fine old Savage 99s with rotary magazines. Finally, I like bolt actions, preferably a Mauser design with its heavy-duty claw extractors. The Ruger Model 77 and the Remington 700 are fine bolt-action rifles.

I never had much use for a semiautomatic rifle when bear hunting. I have tried several and the only one that gave me good service and never let me down was the Browning BAR .338 Magnum. I have no opinion concerning pump guns because I never used one and have never seen any other professional bear hunter use one. This may be due to the fact that I have never hunted bear in the eastern or southern states, where I hear the Remington "trombones" are quite popular.

A Mauser-action rifle with a twenty- or twenty-two-inch barrel is just about right for any bear hunt. I can't tell you what a pain in the backside long barrels are when tracking a big bear through alders, oaks, or willows. Not only are long barrels hard to manage; they are also downright dangerous! If your rifle is equipped with a sling, make sure it has detachable swivels so the sling can be removed when you hunt in dense brush. It is very disconcerting to try to raise your rifle for that much-needed stopping shot and be unable to because its sling is caught on a limb.

A flat British V with a gold or ivory front bead is still about the best sighting device for bear hunting. It's quick, accurate, and highly effective in the semitwilight conditions of heavy-canopied coniferous forests. For the best all-round sights for both close and faraway shots in all weather conditions, it is hard to find a better combination than a Lyman 48 or 57 rear-aperture sight with a gold-face Sourdough front post. It is only slightly less accurate than a scope, and if it is raining or snowing, which it generally is in the bear country of the Pacific Northwest, that combination is easy to clear by blowing through the aperture. Indeed, I have found that blowing through the aperture clears the sights instantly, so no time is wasted wiping a fogged or rain-splattered scope lens before getting off the shot.

If your eyes aren't quite what they used to be, scopes are certainly worth their weight in gold. Scopes made by established companies will usually work OK, but try to avoid the real cheapies. You generally get what you pay for. It can be very hazardous to your well-being if you are charged by a grizzly and can find no cross hairs in your scope. Many adequate bear calibers have a tendency to jar the reticles right out of the scope after a few rounds.

Also avoid variable scopes over four power. Above four power you will see nothing but fur at close range, and when the scope is set on long range it will induce you to try a shot that is not practical. It is my personal choice not to use a variable power scope. I know you might think that that is ridiculous, arguing that variable scopes are really the "cat's meow" since they allow for close shots as well as long ones. Dear reader, I might listen to your sales pitch if variables were limited to something like one-and-a-half to four power, but anything above that is not to be considered. It is just a matter of time before you have your scope turned to maximum magnification for a long-range shot and forget to lower it upon entering the woods, where if a shot is taken it will have to be a close one. You say you won't forget? Don't bet on it. I have heard people say this and then make that very mistake. When hunters are in the field, what they plan and what they do are often two entirely different things.

On a recent trip to Alaska, I was talking to four Alaska brown bear guides at a Palmer, Alaska, sportsman show. All of them agreed that the use of variable power scopes for potentially dangerous game was number three on the "not to do" list. (Number one was hunting with an inadequate caliber and number two was poor bullet placement.) Remember, Murphy is alive and well and never takes a day off. If there is a way to screw up, you'll do it when hunting dangerous game. How does the hunter get around Murphy's Law? I did it by playing it safe. I never used a variable on something that bites back.

I realize that the next statement is dated, but my absolutely favorite bear scopes were the old steel-tube Weaver K-2.5s, K-3s, and K-4s. What they lacked in optics they more than made up for in sturdiness and dependability.

I will now consider the cartridges and calibers adequate for the taking of blacks, inland grizzlies, and coastal brownies. There is always a lot of discussion about what caliber is capable of killing a bear with one shot. Rather than discuss each caliber, I will make some general comments I hope will be helpful.

First, I will examine the marginal calibers. One of my favorites for hunting mule deer, mountain sheep, and antelope is the .25-06 in either its standard or improved casing. I have killed three or four black bear with it using 115-grain bullets or larger. But despite the fact that all the kills had been made with one shot, I consider the caliber barely marginal for blacks and totally inappropriate for grizzly. Remember what happened in chapter 13—Dick's .25 caliber and my .264 were not sufficient on the blond bear.

While the .25-06 is only marginal on black bear, the 7mm Remington Magnum is a fine killer of blacks or any other bear up to six hundred pounds, but it is not a stopper. If you spot a black bear feeding in the open—presenting a clear broadside shot and not at all aggressive—the 7mm Remington Magnum will kill it like lightning if a 160-grain Nosler is placed in the center of the bear's shoulder at spine level. Take that same bear and shoot it twice in the guts with that same rifle. The bear will lie in a dense oak patch nursing its injury, or it will charge filled with adrenaline. You'd better have something besides the 7mm to stop its final rush. Hits from the 7mm will not knock the bear off its feet, much less put it down for good. I have seen bears take hits from the .270, 7mm, and .300 class of rifles squarely in the chest and be no more inconvenienced than if stung by a horsefly.

At 100 yards, the 7mm Remington Magnum loaded with 154-grain bullets will deliver about the same energy as the .338 Winchester Magnum firing 250-grain bullets. But foot/pounds does not tell the whole story. The .338 has almost double the stopping power of the 7mm Remington Magnum. Furthermore, the Winchester .300 Magnum shooting 180-grain bullets over 300 yards has practically the same energy as a .375 H&H Magnum shooting 300-grainers. But there is no comparison between the actual stopping power of the two calibers. The .375 H&H is one of the best calibers for stopping dangerous game.

The .338 is a superior stopper of black bear, very good on inland grizzly, and adequate on Alaska brownies. Though an excellent killer of all three, it is definitely a better stopper on black and inland grizzly than it is on the huge Alaska brown bear.

A friend of mine named John Luster, a Dall sheep and brown bear hunting guide living in Palmer, Alaska, uses a .300 Winchester Magnum as his brown bear backup rifle and loads it with Nosler

Partition bullets. There are probably not many better shots with the .300 than he. But another friend of mine, Mike Horstman from Wasilla, Alaska, will use nothing less for backup than a .375 and is seriously considering replacing that with a .416 Remington or Rigby Magnum. While John knows his stuff, I'll have to go along with Mike in his recommendation for a stopping rifle. Though the .300 is pure poison on blackies, good on inland grizzlies, and more than adequate for coastal browns, it is not a stopper even in the hands of an excellent and cool marksman.

I know this sounds like a lot of gobbledygook for the inexperienced hunter, but I am sure the professionals understand exactly what I am talking about even if they don't all agree with me. Professional guide John Luster is able to handle the situation because of experience. He is cool under pressure and an accurate shooter, and he has a working knowledge of bear anatomy. In other words, John can make a .300 work as a stopper, but very few other hunters can.

There are African hunters who believe there are no real stoppers of dangerous game until you reach .45 bore diameter. Then and only then can you say with some degree of confidence that you have a rifle that is a stopper. Derwin Gore, a friend who lives in Hayden, Colorado, makes a very convincing argument in favor of .45 bore and up. I have a strong tendency to agree with Derwin and my old friend Elmer Keith: The biggest thing you can shoot, and shoot accurately, is what you want to use on the big boys that can hit back.

I do not exactly know why bullets of big-bore size and heavy weight that travel at medium velocities are the splendid stoppers and magnificent killers that they are. But the proof is in the pudding. An example of this occurred in chapter 5. C. E. Barnett's .300 Weatherby smacked the big bear three times squarely on the shoulder but failed to make it stagger, much less put it down. Contrary to what the high velocity enthusiasts would like to have us believe, my sawed-off .358 Winchester shooting 250-grain Silvertips took the bear off its feet on each of its three hits.

Don't let energy figures make a fool of you. Velocity is good on some occasions, and it certainly boosts energy figures. But on the large, adrenaline-filled bear you want a large-bore heavyweight bullet drilling deep into the animal's vitals and breaking bone. That is the only way to stop a charging bear.

For black bear the calibers and bullet densities I recommend are the following:

.270 through .30 calibers, using 150- to 220-grain bullets between 2400 and 2800 fps;

.318 through .375 calibers, using 200- to 300-grain bullets between 2400 and 2600 fps;

.40 through .45 calibers, using 300- to 410-grain bullets between 1600 and 2000 fps.

For inland grizzlies I recommend:

.30 caliber, using 200-grain or larger bullets between 2400 and 2800 fps;

.318 through .375 calibers, using 225- to 300-grain bullets between 2400 and 2600 fps;

.40 through .45 calibers, using 350- to 410-grain bullets between 1800 and 2400 fps.

For Alaska brown bear I recommend:

.338 through .375 calibers, using 250- to 350-grain bullets between 2400 and 2600 fps;

.40 through .45 calibers, using 350- to 510-grain bullets between 2200 and 2400 fps.

You may notice some velocities are relatively low on the higher calibers. I believe velocities on some rifles are way too high on dangerous game, for high velocity can cause bullets to rupture and disintegrate on impact. These bullets are not able to penetrate to the vitals of the prey, as happened in my first three hits on the blond bear described in chapter 13.

What are my four all-time favorite rifles for bear hunting? One of my old standbys is the 22-inch-barrel Pre-'64 Winchester Featherweight .270, propelling 150-grain Nosler Partitions at 2800 fps. It is sighted with a gold-face Sourdough front sight and a Lyman 57 receiver sight, or a K-4 steel-tube Weaver scope. I have never relegated this rifle to a backup. Indeed, I have killed over one hundred bear with the .270, finding it excellent when I was able to pick and precisely place my shots. No bear ever took more than three shots to stop, and no bear ever escaped once I hit it.

The rifle that accompanied me on most of my dangerous bear hunts was the 22-inch-barrel .358 Winchester caliber on a Model 99 Savage with rotary magazine. The rifle fit me extremely well, came to point of aim naturally, had quick action, and always fed with uncanny reliability. It was absolutely lethal with 250-grain Barnes roundnose bullets and did very well with the old 250-grain Winchester Silvertips. It was sighted with a flat-face gold front bead and a flat British V rear sight. I wish I still had that fine little rifle.

Another mighty good rifle was made for me by E. E. Northup, who lived in Colorado Springs, Colorado, and was my lifelong gunsmith. It had a 20-inch Douglas premium barrel screwed into a commercial action, chambered in .338 Winchester Magnum with a custom stock by Bishop. It was equipped with a Sourdough front sight and a Lyman 48 receiver sight. I loaded it with 250-grain Nosler Partitions, 275-grain

Speer roundnose bullets, and 300-grain Winchester Power-Points. I did some really fine work with all three of those loadings. The rifle weighed only 8 pounds, and its superior stock made it a pleasure to shoot.

I was also quite fond of my Pre-'64 .375 H&H Winchester, which had the barrel sawed off to 20 inches and was resighted with a gold Sourdough front sight and a Lyman 48 receiver sight. It was extremely accurate, weighed only 8 pounds, 4 ounces, and, like the other three, was balanced perfectly, coming to a natural point of aim. It was at its best with 300-grain Noslers and 350-grain Barnes roundnose bullets.

Two calibers I am extremely fond of but have limited experience with are the .338-06 and the .35 Whelan. Both, by my criteria, should be excellent calibers for blacks and inland grizzlies and adequate for Alaska browns in the hands of a cool and deliberate marksman. I wish now I had used both calibers more often.

I am not a fan of belted bullet cases when I can get the same performance out of the nonbelted variety. I believe the most common dangerous occurrence when hunting big game is short-stroking the bolt to cause a jam or failure to extract due to broken extractors. It is imperative that one's rifle and ammunition combination be thoroughly checked out for function and reliability before the hunting trip. Your rifle and ammunition combination must feed, fire, extract, and then feed again—every time!—whether the action is operated deliberately or hastily. The trigger and sear adjustment must be set with utmost care. You cannot afford the luxury of recocking the bolt because of a poorly set sear. This adjustment is best left to a competent gunsmith. These are not only my opinions; they are also the opinions of many others who have hunted dangerous game.

I would like to leave you with the following outline of caliber designations and their corresponding fps:

from .270 through .30, 2400-2800 fps;
from .318 through .375, 2400-2600 fps;
from .40   through .45, 2200-2400 fps.

Someday when you have time, study up on the classic cartridges. You will discover that they fall within the schema above.

Handguns for Bears?

If a handgun is used as the primary weapon when bear hunting, it must be in the hands of an expert shooter. The size of the bear will justify the caliber used. The weapon should be easy to handle and capable of firing repeat shots. This would exclude, then, the so-called "hand cannons" normally associated with rifle cartridges.

Also, an adequate cartridge must be near the top of the list of what you look for in a handgun. Several new handgun calibers have placed handguns on a totally different plane. Now available are the .500, .475, and .45 Linebaugh; the .454 Casull and several new .50s that I am not familiar with. All of them have much more power than the old .44 Magnum loadings. The pistols that are made to shoot these calibers are, for the most part, revolvers that offer multiple-hit capacity. I've always liked the idea of having more than one shot available.

High-caliber handguns are not toys, and it takes someone far above the average hunter to shoot them well. These calibers work extremely well on bear over six hundred pounds. Bear below six hundred pounds can be killed by a well-placed shot from a .41 Magnum, .45 Colt, or .44 Magnum.

What is accurate shooting with a handgun? It is when you can put 5 shots in 6 inches at whatever distance you choose. If your capability, for instance, is 5 shots in 6 inches at 35 yards under field conditions, that is pretty good. On the other hand, if you can put only 5 shots in 6 inches at 5 yards, you'd better also have nerves of steel because you are going to be very close to the bruin! When using a handgun as a primary weapon, 5 shots in 6 inches at 35 yards must be the bottom line. Anything less is not good enough.

For most bear hunters, the handgun should be used only as backup, but it does not follow that the hunter need not practice with the weapon. I wonder how many guys go to the woods armed with a handgun, believing it will save their life in an emergency when they couldn't hit the broad side of a barn with it for lack of practice. Often a hunter will spend many hours learning to shoot his rifle accurately but totally neglect practicing with the handgun. Most hunters know it takes practice to shoot well with a rifle but also think the handgun somehow takes on magical properties of its own when the chips are down. As an old hunting guide at Kodiak Island once said to a client: "If you haven't practiced with that pistol, buddy, make sure that the revolver is free from all protuberances because it will sure hurt when that big grizzly puts it where the sun don't shine." As a general rule, guides do not appreciate a hunter who has no idea of the capability of his weapon—rifle or pistol.

I asked that guide if he thought a handgun was a good weapon to carry. "By all means!" he said. "It will do to commit suicide with just before the bear grabs you!" Well, I have more respect than that for the handgun, but the old-timer made his point. Don't take the handgun to the woods until you have practiced, practiced, practiced!

A .357 is a very poor killer of any size bear. The only way that caliber could put a bear out of commission is with a brain shot. Of course, a number of bears have been killed by .38 specials, 9mm, and .38 supers or their equivalent, but they are still not acceptable defense weapons against bears.

I never–*never*–go to the woods without my .45 Linebaugh or .44 Magnum Model 29 Smith & Wesson. Call me chicken if you like, but I will not be the victim of a bear attack without putting up a fight. A bear will almost always wind up with your hand in its mouth. You just need to make sure that the one it grabs has a pistol in it. I can think of six cases where the bear was killed instead of the hunter when at the last possible second the big pistol went off in its mouth.

Personally, I never used a pistol as a primary weapon. I know how hard a bear can be to kill using a heavy-caliber rifle, and I do not believe that any pistol will accomplish what a rifle will in caliber .338, .375, or .416. I always carried a pistol when I hunted bear. I felt a real sense of added security knowing I had with me a large caliber handgun that I knew how to shoot.

Primary or secondary? You decide. But whatever you prefer, practice with the handgun until you have reached a very high level of proficiency.

Bullets and Proper Placement

Where do I shoot the bear to deliver the killing shot? What are the best bullets to use when hunting bear? I have been asked these two questions, so closely related to each other, many times during my life. I will try to answer them in this chapter.

It is important that the hunter have a working knowledge of bear anatomy if he expects to stop the animal with one shot. He must know the bear's skeletal structure, muscle development, nervous system, and the location of vital organs. To shoot at a bear without first knowing the best place to shoot it is extremely dangerous and might possibly end tragically for the hunter.

Where should you shoot the bear? The answers to this question are easy to state but difficult to carry out in the field. Your best hits are to the bear's brain and spinal cord, though even these hits do not always kill the animal immediately. I have seen bears with spine severed and bullet wounds to the brain live several seconds before the lights went out. Hits that miss these areas will usually fail to drop the animal in its tracks.

It is not easy to hit a bear's brain. Take the time to go to a museum or taxidermy shop to examine a bear's skull. You will discover that the only way to get a bullet into its brain without first hitting a sloping surface of bone is through the nasal passage.

In chapter 2, you'll remember, I hit Old Griz's skull, but obliquely, causing the shot to glance off and the bear to charge. I don't know about you, but I find it a little difficult to put a bullet directly in the end of a bear's snout, especially when it is charging at speeds somewhere between thirty and forty miles per hour. Though I have made a couple of those shots—and they certainly are fun to talk about with your hunting buddies—I would be perfectly happy to have never had to make them.

The bear's brain is located toward the rear of and high up in the cranial cavity. When the bear is in a quartering position, the brain can be hit at the intersection of two imaginary lines: One line runs vertically through the base of the skull to the atlas (first) vertebra, and the second line runs horizontally from the eye to the base of the ear. If you set your sights or cross hairs on that area, you will have a brain hit. If the shot strikes below the horizontal line, you will have a very angry bear.

When trying to hit the brain with a broadside shot, you should aim one inch below the base of the ear, which is about horizontal to the eye socket. A frontal shot should be taken from a kneeling position (so that you are level with the animal) and be directed at the eye or snout, and a rear shot at the intersection of spine and skull. But because the brain is difficult to hit, I do not recommend it as a target—especially if the bear is in motion—unless it is the only shot left that might save your life.

The next best thing to an instant kill is instant incapacitation. The best shot to achieve this is directed at the center of the off shoulder at spine level. If you use the right caliber and right bullet, your problem will be solved. A bear with both shoulders broken and a severed spine is down for the count.

One of my favorites is a rear-quartering shot. The bullet drives on a straight line from the point of entry to the off shoulder.

However, it can be accomplished only with a high-caliber rifle driving a high-grained bullet with good sectional density and of heavy construction. This combination will ensure enough penetration to smash the bone of the off shoulder. If you try this shot with a small-caliber, high-velocity rifle, the bullet could disintegrate on impact or drive in but not make it through the chest cavity. Such a shot is next to worthless.

If you have a front-quartering shot, it is very difficult to hit the bear's off shoulder. I recommend breaking the ball joint of the shoulder, which will leave the bear with three legs, definitely hampering its locomotion. The ball joint also makes a good target because it is the size of a baseball. Another good shot is to the spine, which can be hit with a rear or rear-quartering shot. It drops the bear like lightning. The best spine shot is to the back of the neck, an area two and a half inches wide and three inches long. If the bear is moving directly away from you, a bullet placed just above the root of the tail will shatter the spine and drop the bear immediately, but only if a high caliber is used. Small calibers are not capable of delivering a killing shot to areas of big bone. Remember, big bone must not only be hit; it must be pulverized. If you have enough rifle—such as a .416 Remington, Rigby, or Weatherby—shots directed into the center pelvic girdle will bring down the largest of bears.

If using a small caliber, you will not have enough power to break down the bear's skeletal structure. You must rely on either hemorrhaging or suffocation to kill the bear before it has time to charge, and you will almost certainly need to take more than one shot. Nevertheless, I have used small calibers to kill several bear with one shot by hitting the high-lung area from broadside. I did this by following a vertical line up the bear's front leg into the body cavity.

A high-lung shot, which suffocates, will kill a still-mobile bear in forty to a hundred yards. If standing still when hit, the bear will drop in its tracks only about 20 percent of the time. The shot is a sure killer but not necessarily a quick one.

If the bottom of the lungs is punctured, instead of suffocating the bear will die from hemorrhaging. It may travel up to a mile, however, before going down for the count. If you hit only one lung, you may never find the bear. If you miss the lungs by shooting high, you may still sever the spine; if you miss low, you may hit the heart. The heart shot is a sure killer. Contrary to popular belief, though, it does not necessarily kill quickly. On one occasion I watched a large black bear run one hundred forty yards with its heart literally blown to fragments throughout its chest cavity.

With either a high-lung or heart shot, the time from the infliction of the wound to the animal's demise may be from ten seconds to four minutes, depending on how much damage has been done and the exact location of the wound. You can readily understand that if the bear is bent on mayhem, it will have plenty of time to accomplish it. It is wise, then, to shoot at vital organs only if you do not have sufficient caliber to immobilize the bear by breaking down its skeletal structure.

Bullet experts like to recommend bullets that remain in the animal's body rather than exiting. Their contention is that energy is wasted if the bullet exits the body because it reduces the shock to the animal. But this is more true of elk than of bear. When hunting in temperatures below 32 degrees Fahrenheit, greater shock is caused to the elk when the bullet exits the body than when it enters. Ask any elk hunter about his quickest kills. He will tell you they occurred when the bullet exited the prey. Experienced cold-climate hunters want the bullet to exit, for they know that an exit hole not only leaves a blood trail to use for tracking; it also allows cold air to flood the chest cavity.

Nevertheless, I have seen bear and elk take hits from .270 to .300 caliber rifles. Though the shot hit both lungs, not one drop of blood could be found from the prey. I discovered that the skin around the exit wound often seals immediately, like a cork on a bottle, leaving no blood trail to track or hole for the cold to enter.

I want the bullet to enter the bear at any angle and exit, but not because I think the exit hole will induce shock. A hunter laboring under the delusion that he will shock a bear to death had better see a psychiatrist before going bear hunting. Bullet experts may be correct that energy is wasted when the bullet exits, but I for one am not concerned about the waste of energy. There are only three things the hunter needs to accomplish: the breaking down of the skeletal structure, the disruption of the nervous system, and the inducing of hemorrhaging through lacerations to the body tissue. It doesn't take a physicist to calculate that a bullet that does not have the power to exit has absolutely no chance of breaking the near shoulder, pulverizing the spine in between, and smashing the off shoulder. In truth, a bullet that doesn't exit from the chest cavity seldom gets past the near shoulder before totally disintegrating. A broadside shot that misses big bone or the vitals and does not exit is pretty much worthless. The shot needs to break bone, but it also needs to strike at any angle and exit. What bullet should the hunter use to help him accomplish this?

Bullet manufacturers will tell you that their bullets are the very best money can buy. What they don't often tell you is the game on which to use the bullet. The 100-grain bullet in .270 caliber will absolutely cream coyote or woodchuck, but what will it do against an angry five-hundred-pound grizzly?

What bullet would give you the most confidence when shooting a thousand-pound grizzly through the shoulders with a .300 Winchester Magnum? Would you rather be using a 150-grain Hornady Spire-Point or a 200-grain Nosler Partition? If you said the 150, go back to the drawing board! Do not misunderstand what I say. I am not saying a 150-grain Hornady isn't a good bullet. It will kill mountain sheep or mule deer like lightning, but it will seldom if ever do the job on a large grizzly. Remember, match your bullets to your game and to exactly what you want to accomplish.

Strictly speaking, when it comes to shooting bear there are only a few bullets that I recommend without hesitation. I realize that in the last few years great strides have been made in making bullets, but I will not endorse the new bullets since I have not used them.

The bullets I have had the most success using are Nosler Partitions and Barnes Dangerous Game bullets. I have never recovered a 250-grain Nosler Partition .338 bullet from any black bear I have ever shot, for it has always exited. This is also true of the thick-jacketed Barnes roundnose Big Game bullets of a weight of at least 250 grains. Total penetration with terrific damage to the internals of the beast before exiting has been a consistent trademark of both Nosler and Barnes bullets. The 150- and 160-grain .270 Noslers and the old 170-grain roundnose Barnes are also good bullets, with penetration comparable to that of the .338. Two other Barnes bullets that are great on elk and bear but often overlooked are the 250-grain in .300 caliber and the 350-grain in .375 caliber.

My friend Derwin Gore has had the same success using 250-grain Nosler Partitions in his .338-06 as I have had using the bullet in a .338 Winchester Magnum. Elmer Keith told me years ago that he was perfectly satisfied with his 275-grain WTC bullets and Barnes bullets in his .35 Whelan. The WTC is no longer manufactured, but the Barnes bullets in 250, 275, and 300 grains are still alive and well.

It is extremely important for a bullet to maintain its original path through the animal after impact. In my opinion, the roundnose parallel-sided bullets with sectional density do this better than any other bullet. The spire-pointed bullets, on the other hand, have a tendency to be deflected at their first encounter with massive bone. I know there are other good bullets on the market, but the roundnose parallel-sided bullets are the only ones I have used with a near 100 percent success rate.

Before closing this chapter I would like to add a thought or two concerning solids, which are bullets that feature a solid copper, nickel, or steel jacket with no lead exposed. I constantly hear people say that a solid bullet is worthless because it doesn't expand and so ends up zipping through the prey without doing much internal damage. I wonder if they understand for what purpose the solid is used.

Some varmint shooters use them to inflict the least amount of damage to valuable hides. Though these particular solids are great for small game, they should not be used for big game because they are easily deflected upon hitting large bone. In general, the only solid bullet used by American hunters is the small-caliber, high-velocity pointed-tip version, which has also been used by the military.

Having said that, I will probably shock the bear-hunting novice by adding that I would really like to see made legal again roundnose parallel-sided solid bullets of .338 diameter or more for the hunting of bear in the United States. Remember, the bullet needs to penetrate to the vitals or break large bone. Solid bullets of high-caliber designations accomplish this extremely well. Pay no attention to those who say solids just punch little holes in the prey without creating much tissue damage. Wrong! Any caliber .338 and higher shooting roundnose or flatnose solids creates wound channels of a uniformity and depth seldom produced by softnose expanding bullets. The person who says solids aren't killers is probably not familiar with the high-caliber solids.

By sticking to the principles outlined in the last three chapters, taken from my many years of hunting big game, you will be taking a giant step toward becoming an effective big-game hunter. Quite possibly it will keep you from making errors commonly committed by the inexperienced. Bear hunting can be terribly dangerous, and what you learn here may someday save your life or the life of a companion. Good hunting!